A Dreaming Spires R

REVISED: How to Ace the CIE 0500 English Language IGCSE (Higher Tier)

Eight Lessons to Get a Grip!
2019 Syllabus

Copyright © 2018 by Dr K E Patrick
All rights reserved. This book or any portion thereof
may not be reproduced or used in any manner whatsoever
without the express written permission of the publisher
except for the use of brief quotations in a book review.

First Printing, 2016; Revised edition 2018

CONTENTS

Foreword	v
Additional Foreword to the 2019 Edition	ix
Before You Begin …	xiii
1. Lesson One	1
2. Lesson Two	12
3. Lesson Three	28
4. Lesson Four	48
5. Lesson Five	62
6. Lesson Six	74
7. Lesson Seven	88
8. Lesson Eight	109
9. Bonus Mini-Lesson	121
About the Author	125
Appendix A	127
Answers and Notes	131

Foreword

Hello and welcome to this new and revised eight-week revision course to help prepare for the CIE 0500 English Language IGCSE (higher tier) exam, as found in their 2019 syllabus. *If you are preparing for the exam for October 2018, you will need the first edition, which we call the "Blue" edition because its cover is blue.*

This revision guide is a book-format version of the popular crammer course taught online as Dreaming Spires Revision. It is not affiliated with the Cambridge International Examinations board in any way, but it contains observations, tips, and ideas based on my experience as one of their examiners and many years as a private tutor.

Normally, I don't like teaching to an exam. I think it does a disservice to any subject. However, as I was marking exam after exam one year, I observed that there were mistakes that students were making that cropped up again and again. I started creating a list of do's and don'ts[1] which grew over time into an online revision course, and finally, into this little printed booklet.

It just seemed that, if students were going to be taking this exam, they deserved to know the best way to do it.

Besides, I've come to accept that in education — as in any journey — students need to not only buy the ticket, but they probably want to buy one that's the most direct route as well.

> ***This revision guide is like going "as the crow flies" on your journey:***
> ***as direct a route as you can get!***

Here, you will find tips and tricks that will help you manage your stress, your time, and your approach. Therefore, you should do better on the exam once you've worked through these exercises.

Of course, there are no guarantees. People underperform for so many reasons — bad time management, failure to read the question, preparing only the exam papers rather than learning the general skills, or just blind panic.

This guide is here to minimise such mistakes and help you toward the best exam answers you can make. I admit it's rough around the edges, this book, but the information is what matters; I hope you can forgive the idiosyncratic formatting!

Finally, you might want to pop on over to Facebook and get connected with other students who are using this revision guide, past students of the online courses, or even yours truly. Communication is key. We might not solve the world's problems, but hopefully we'll crack the revision approach to 0500 together.

Many regards,

Dr P

Additional Foreword to the 2019 Edition

Before we go any further, I just wanted to explain in simple terms how the 2019 syllabus differs from the one from 2015 2018.

The changes are minor, but significant enough to warrant a new revision guide. If you pick up a past paper from the previous syllabus, you'll see that the exam papers designated as 21, 22, or 23 have two parts to Question 3, called 3a and 3b.

In these papers, Question 3a wanted a 15-point list of information from an unseen passage, and Question 3b wanted the candidate to turn these points into a fluent summary, written in the candidate's own words.

For the 2019 series, the exam board has dropped 3a — the 15-point list — and wants students to just write points as the summary as in 3b.

It's a change that I applaud; having two separate questions for essentially the same material seemed redundant. In practice, however, students will still create a list of points to put into a summary, so what used to be 3a and part of the mark scheme will now be the pre-writing note-taking stage.

The good news is that, even though there is a slight change to the exam for next year, the remainder of the past papers will be exactly the same, so they're still useful for preparation.

This is why I still use the 2015 past paper as an example, and am simply going to modify my instruction for Question 3 to reflect this change.

In fact, the exam board's own specimen paper for the new 2019 "spec" ("specification") is a modified paper from the Winter Series in 2015. It would probably be very useful for you to print out both versions and compare them. I have made them available for you in one pdf document at the following link: https://tinyurl.com/yd2rbpkh.

Another activity that students find really useful for preparing for the exam is signing up for my 7-hour crammer course at Dreaming Spires Revision. In this course, we go over the questions in the same way as in this guide, but with new examples. I also set and mark homework, including a mock exam. If you've found this book helpful, you might consider grabbing a place on one of my upcoming crammers, taught live and online. Then, you can truly say you've done everything you can possibly do to help your teen get ready for this exam!

All the best!

Kat

Before You Begin ...

To Students: Before you begin, you need to "KNOW" ...

KNOW that there's no rush.

First of all, if you have bought this book before you know how to write a good sentence, use paragraphs, spell reasonably well, write with a decent vocabulary; before you have read a lot of good books; and before you have some maturity (usually, but not always, this is after you're 14), then I think you should really go away and practise, read, and live a bit more.

It sounds harsh, but remember — I'm an examiner of this exam. I read hundreds of scripts every year, and I can tell when someone is too young. Their skills are too weak, their knowledge is limited, and they will have been penalised simply for sitting this exam too soon. The bulk of students sitting this exam are 15 or 16, maybe even 17, so I believe you may be taking an unnecessary risk if you take it earlier than that.

So, in my opinion, you should wait. It will only do you favours!

KNOW that there's due diligence involved on your part.

You can buy this book and never crack it open. Or you can thumb through it. Or you can work on it for just an hour or so. However, if you're serious about your studies, you will set aside regular time to concentrate, practise, and expect to learn something. That's "due diligence" – it won't work if you just put the book under your pillow and hope the info seeps in!

Whichever option you choose — the easy way or the hard way — it makes no difference to me. Once you've bought it, I've got my reward for the work I've put into this guide for you.

Your reward comes in August or January, depending on when you've taken the exam, because that's when your grades come out.

I don't know about you, but my personal feeling is that I'd like to know I did my very best when I open that list of marks and see what I made. I would be very cross with myself if I thought I could have done better, if only I'd worked a bit harder in the run up to the exam.

KNOW that there are expectations.

Finally, I require all my revision students to commit to a regular homework regime of basic skills. Decide for me right now that you're going to do this, on your own, regularly and diligently.

Are you ready to make that decision?

Assuming you said yes, then you have committed to improving your test-taking skills and writing ability in a way that will make you a better student and, yes, even a better person.

Expectation one:

Four times a week, you will copy out this sentence:

It is as important to read and understand the question as it is to read and understand the unseen reading passages.

I refer to this as the "memory verse." When students bomb a question on this exam, it's usually because they didn't read the question carefully enough.

Over the years, my former students come back to tell me that this was such a great bit of advice, and that memorising this verse has served them well in all their subjects and all their exams.

So, during this eight-week revision course that you're committing to here, you will write this verse down 36 times. Get one of those little exercise books from WHSmith and keep it only for this purpose.

Expectation two:

Another regular task you will do four times a week is called copywork. This is a Charlotte Mason method staple (Charlotte Mason being a Victorian educator with progressive ideas about education that really worked!), but it's also crucial you do this for the exam — it will improve your vocabulary, sentence structures, punctuation, and reading comprehension. The sooner you get started, the more effect it will have on your writing style.

Here's the task: choose a really good book, like Dickens' A Tale of Two Cities, or Lord of the Rings, or anything else that's really dense and wordy. Set your timer for ten minutes, and then carefully copy a passage word for word, making sure every word is spelled correctly and every punctuation mark is perfect.

Over time, you will probably find that you can hold four or five words in your head at a time as you copy them out, but just remember: this is supposed to be ten minutes of perfection. Don't rush, and don't lose concentration.

Expectation three:

In Lesson One, you will see something called "narration" — this is just a summary of what you've read, but it works on the deep-memory of your brain and makes it "stick" more. Getting in the habit of narrating everything you read will contribute to a stronger understanding of the unseen passages you get in the exam. As part of exam technique, I suggest that students read a paragraph of the passage, jot a little marginal marker about what it said, and move on to the next one to repeat the process.

If you start using this technique for EVERYTHING you read — whether it's science textbooks, novels, or the newspaper — it will help you improve your attentiveness while you're reading, and thus improve your comprehension.

Summary:

So, you have now committed to doing three things on a regular basis: copying the memory verse 4 times a week, doing 10 minutes of copywork for 4 days a week, and narrating everything you read regardless of the subject.

These three tasks, performed regularly and diligently, will be the first thing that sets you apart from 99% of the students who sit this exam.

Don't you want to be in the top 1% before you even sit down in the exam centre???? Of course you do!

Finally:

There are occasional exercises in each lesson, demarcated by the instruction "DO" and followed by a little symbol that looks like this:

DO NOT PROCEED
Without doing the task first

Image from Pixabay

As he says, **you are not to proceed any further** in the book until you have done the task. Revision isn't revision if you just read through it — you have to put into practice what I'm telling you, or you might as well have bought two tall vanilla lattes and a slice of cheesecake from Starbucks instead of spending the money on this book (instead, I'll be buying the lattes BECAUSE you bought this book — thank you very much). Seriously: do the exercises.

How to Use this Book

Ideally, you will work through this revision guide over a eight-week period. I think there's too much to take on board if you try to do it faster, and sometimes you just need to let ideas, skills, and advice sink in before trying to add more ideas, skills, and advice into the mix. Each of the eight sessions is set out in the same format: a review, a quiz, an overview, a look at something specific, and revision suggestions.

I strongly advise that you get a blank book and actually take notes from the guide. Studies show that students learn best by writing notes by hand because it requires more connections in the brain, and thus helps you remember the information better.

Now, an apology: I'm sorry that there is a blurred-out image or two in the guide. No, there's nothing wrong with your eyes, and there's nothing wrong with my printer. I've had to blur out the images because they belong to CIE, and I don't have the legal right to reproduce them. I can only give you the impression of what they say or look like, so you will need to print out a copy of the exam papers yourself. My suggestion is that you look on somewhere like papacambridge.com. Print these out so you have them to refer to. At the time that I wrote this, you can find the insert, question paper, and mark scheme for June 2015 Paper 22 here: https://tinyurl.com/y7ot4xa9

While on the subject of copyright, please note that this book is copyrighted, too. That means that you don't have any right to reproduce this guide, print it out, or share it, so please respect that in an honourable way. The photos, too, are mine, unless noted otherwise.

Now, that's enough preliminary chit-chat; let's get started, and good luck!

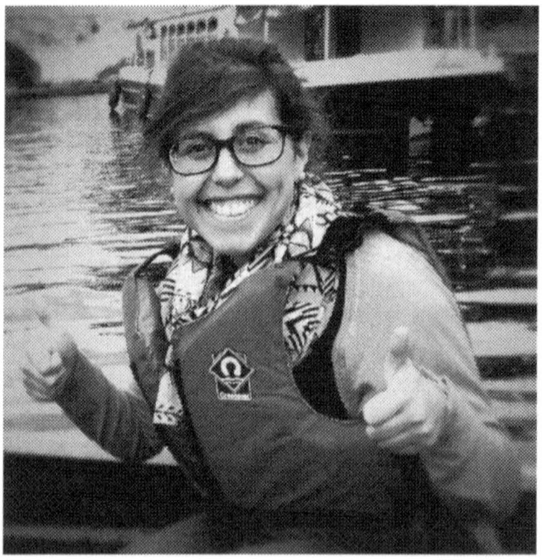

Lesson One

As we start this 8-week revision course, I want to set the record straight about something. I don't actually believe in the old proverb "practice makes perfect".

Just think of how many ways you could disprove that. Say I play the piano, and I plink-plonk away at the keys for 2 hours a day, blissfully unaware that my version of Für Elise is missing the all-important D-sharp. All I've done is made my imperfection permanent. in other words, **practice doesn't make perfect; it makes permanent!**

What I mean in terms of your revision is that you shouldn't rush this process, but take your time in learning the basics and the underlying principles. You will then have a firm grasp of what's expected. The more you practise slowly at first, getting everything right from the beginning, the more confidence you'll gain, and eventually, the faster you'll be able to manage the exam paper.

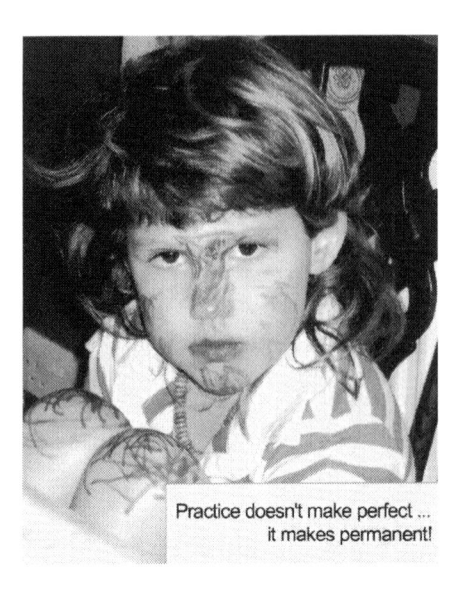

Practice doesn't make perfect ... it makes permanent!

0500 Higher Tier at a Glance

The English (First Language) IGCSE exam is made up of three papers, each with various codes. Paper 1 is the Core Level paper; I don't cover it in this course. I do cover the other two papers – generically, they're known as 0500-02 and 0500-03, but you are probably taking 0500-22 and 0500-31. Papers can also be coded 21 or 23, 32 or 33. This is because the exam board creates several different versions, so those in countries with different time zones can take their exam without spoiling the questions for those who haven't even woken up yet!

There's also an exam taken by students in India in February/March of each year, also with the codes 0500-22 and

-32. If you can find a copy of them on the internet, they're useful for revising and taking as a mock.

The difference between the two papers is the emphasis: Paper 2 is the READING paper, and Paper 3 is the WRITING paper.

Don't think for a minute that you don't need to do any writing in Paper 2, nor any reading in Paper 3. That's not what I mean at all. It's simply a matter of emphasis. Paper 2 is more concerned with your reading comprehension, ability to read between the lines, and understanding of how language works; Paper 3 is more concerned with your ability to organise your writing and demonstrate some level of skill in terms of vocabulary, punctuation, spelling, and the like.

We'll look more at the writing paper starting in Lesson 5. Until then, we'll focus on the reading paper — more specifically, the 0500-22 from the summer 2015 exam.

GENERAL POINTS ABOUT the 0500-22 (or other Paper 2 versions)

0500-22 is the reading paper and contains TWO PARTS:

- Part One refers to Passage A from the insert, and is comprised of two questions.
- Part Two refers to Passage B from the insert, and is one question.

That's THREE questions in total, based on TWO unseen passages. You are required to answer ALL THREE questions.

DO: Look at the front page of your question paper and notice where it says "Answer ALL questions in the space provided." Underline that and write "All" in the margin with an arrow to the same word.

DO NOT PROCEED
Without doing the task first

The first part of the paper is based on Passage A from the insert:

- Question 1: a writing task to prove you understand the passage and can use the information to change audience and purpose.
- Question 2: a task of analysis to prove you can understand how language works.

Key idea = careful reading

LESSON ONE

The second part of the paper is based on Passage B:

- Question 3: write a summary of the key points as stated in the task, using your own words.

Key idea = Choices!

NOTE: Question 3 needs you to really pay attention to what topic it's asking you to pull out of Passage B. This is where your Memory Verse training comes in handy.

Remember the memory verse from "How to Use this Book"?

DETAILED STUDY OF 0500-22 from Summer 2015

(hopefully, you have printed this already from the link at the end of the "Before you Begin" section, on the page before the picture of the "thumbs-up girl".)

- We are going to look at Passage A
- We are going to talk about the best way to gain understanding about the passages in the inserts. This is a fundamental step that many students miss out.
- We will talk about Question 1 specifically in Lesson 2.

DO: Read through Passage A from the insert about Zelda and Bob's canal holiday.

DO NOT PROCEED
Without doing the task first

After reading that passage, I want to go over how you should tackle these inserts. Basically, you're going to start off by summarising what you read.

In the "Before you Begin" section, I explained about "narration" under Expectation Three, and that's what you are going to do with your unseen passages.

"Narration" is simply a telling back of what you've read. It sounds so easy, but the process your brain goes through is such that you remember a passage much better if you put into words what you've been reading. This is so much more successful a way of remembering than having short-answer quizzes or multiple choice.

So let's try it. I am NOT assuming you'll be any good at this if you've never done it before. However, I KNOW that you will be jolly good at it by the time the exam comes around, because you are going to practise doing it as part of your revision for this exam, and for every exam or subject you're studying now.

LESSON ONE

DO: Read the first two paragraphs of Passage A from the insert, and then, <u>without looking at the passage any more,</u> write down a summary of the paragraphs in your notebook.

DO NOT PROCEED
Without doing the task first

It's very important that you don't look back at the passage. You are trying to teach yourself to *attend to* the passage as you read it, rather than being lazy and referring back to it as a crutch.

After you have done this activity, you may go to the "Answers and Notes" section at the back of the book and read my version.[2]

That's what a normal narration looks like. But for the exam, you're not actually going to do a "normal" narration. You don't have time. Instead, you're going to make use of something I call **"marginal markers"**.

Marginal markers are very short narrations — say, a word or a phrase — that you'll jot down next to each paragraph as a way of reminding yourself what each paragraph is about. This will help you find things faster when you're writing your answers.

At the same time, it serves as additional comprehension for yourself as you read through the unseen passages on the insert.

Mini-narrations, in other words.

Here's an example:

DO: Now you make marginal markers in the rest of Passage A from the insert.

After you've read Passage A and gone back through to make

your marginal markers, set Passage A aside where you can't see it anymore.

DO: In your notebook without Passage A in front of you, summarise the whole of Passage A in one or two sentences.

DO NOT PROCEED
Without doing the task first

After you have done this, then you can look at my example in the back of the book.[3]

DON'T PANIC: NARRATE FIRST
*After all, it IS a **reading** exam!*

- *Important Tip: You won't believe how many mistakes can be avoided in exams if students just get these basic facts right — that is, what the story is actually saying. By jotting your narration notes in the margin ("marginal markers"), you will benefit in two ways:*

    - *Cutting down on exam panic*
    - *Getting key details right*

In Lesson One, you've learned:

- The CIE IGCSE exam comes in two parts:

    - Paper 0500-21/22/23 is the reading paper
    - Paper 0500-31/32/33 is the writing paper

- Reading and understanding the question is as important as reading/understanding the unseen passage.
- Narrating your unseen passages by using marginal markers will help you understand the unseen passage before you start writing about it. It will also calm you down.

Revision Suggestions from Lesson One: Copywork

1. Copywork is the easiest, most organic way to learn

vocabulary, spelling, sentence construction, and all the other things connected to good writing.
2. You need good vocabulary, spelling, sentence structure, etc, for the CIE IGCSE English exams.
3. Therefore, you need to start doing copywork.

Basically, copywork is to writing what the "still life" is to painting – the basic building-block that all experts begin with before moving on to better things.

In practical terms, you choose a very well-written book and copy passages from it. Little and often is what's important.

For this course, you should ideally do copywork every day, taking just ten minutes for the task.

DO: Go to the Appendix and read the document called "About Copywork." You will find suggestions for good books to use for this task. Choose one and start to incorporate copywork into your daily routine, spending ten minutes for at least four days a week on this important habit.

Final assignment for Lesson One

DO: In your notebook, narrate what you learned in Lesson One. Remember, narration is a <u>closed book</u> skill, so don't review the lesson or refer back to the book. This is about strengthening your reading memory, so if you cheat and look, you're only making it harder to get ready for the exam.

Lesson Two

In this lesson, we're going to turn our attention to Question 1 on the "Reading" paper, or 0500-21/22/23. We will be referring to the June 0500-22 paper, so you need to have it in front of you during this lesson.

First, let's review what we did in Lesson One.

- We looked at the overview of the exam. It's delivered in two parts: 0500-22 (the reading paper) and 0500-31 (the writing paper).
- We looked at 0500-22 and discovered it consists of 2 unseen passages and three questions, all of which are meant to be answered.
- We learned a memory passage which is to be copied every day, we learned about narration and writing marginal markers, and we had our first exposure to Passage A.

- You were assigned the task of writing marginal markers for Passage A (and getting into the habit of doing this for all revision, whatever the subject), copying the memory verse, and starting daily copywork.

0500-21/22/23 Question One at a Glance

Passage A in the insert has two corresponding questions for it in the question paper: Question 1 and Question 2.

Today, we are focusing on Question 1. To get a feel for the kind of question it is, refer to your copy of 0500-22 right now.

DO: Read through the question on Page 2 of the question paper 0500-22. In your notebook, jot down your first impressions of what it seems to want, how hard it might be, what you might want to include or leave out. These notes don't have to be in complete sentences.

DO NOT PROCEED
Without doing the task first

It's at this stage in the exam when you need your memory passage the most; that is, when reading the question. What is the memory passage? Say it out loud to yourself. If you don't remember it yet, look it up and read it out loud. <u>Don't skip this step: it's important.</u>

Here are some of my observations about this question

1. There are three parts to the answer — bullet points which I will call A1, A2, and A3, because that's how the examiner will notate them when marking your answer.

2. The form, style, voice, and tone of it is that of a letter to a brother.

- *Important Tip: There's no need to get over-zealous about this! It's just a "construct" to get you to change your viewpoint from Zelda to Bob, and to pick out details from the passage from his eyes. Remember that the main point is to show off your reading skills — not to write in a chatty way to your brother about how his wife is doing or other irrelevancies. That just wastes precious time!*

3. Use your own words (don't copy phrases).

DO: On your copy of the question paper, circle or underline the instructions that correspond to my observations 1, 2, and 3 above.

LESSON TWO

DO NOT PROCEED
Without doing the task first

Let's look at these 3 observations more closely.

1. There are three parts to the answer. As though you are Bob, you should write about:

- A1 = your expectations before the trip
- A2 = your feelings about Zelda's behaviour
- A3 = what happened during the rest of the trip; these details are NOT in Passage A, but there are CLUES in the passage that you should use when writing this section.

A1

DO: Look at the first two paragraphs of Passage A and see if you can pick out any details for the A1 portion of the answer; that is, what Bob was expecting from the trip. Write these down in your notebook.

From the first paragraph, you might have picked up that Bob intended the trip to be a "treat," that it would offer peace and quiet, and the suggestion that it's in the country might make you think that it's a break from the city.

From the second paragraph, you might have noted that Bob thought the pastime was "popular," so you could infer he thought he'd see people; that it would be a sociable holiday. The way he's so attentive to boat lingo might suggest to you that he expects to learn a new skill; that it's educational.

DO: Look over my suggestions again and circle the key words in Passage A that link to my ideas. Notice how I take the surface meaning of Zelda's words and "read between the lines," picking up that Bob has heard about the popularity of boating and, by extension, would be expecting to meet people during the trip. This is a higher level of reading than simply identifying the reference to "peace" and "quiet" in paragraph one.

DO NOT PROCEED
Without doing the task first

A2

Now it's time to move on to A2. This is more tricky, because Passage A is written from Zelda's viewpoint, but your answer has to be from Bob's. You will have to work hard to **infer** what Bob felt about Zelda's behaviour. This is a two-stage process. First, what did Zelda do? Second, how might Bob feel about that action?

In Passage A, look at the paragraph that begins "All this took too long."

DO: Write a short narration of what Bob does in this paragraph. Then write what Zelda does. What do you think Bob might have felt about what Zelda did?

DO NOT PROCEED
Without doing the task first

To my mind, this paragraph is one where Bob is really "getting into" the whole boating scene. He isn't just listening patiently to the old gentleman as he rabbits on about boating; Bob is actually "plying" him with questions, meaning that he is asking again and again for further information. Bob is really keen on this whole thing.

And Zelda? She is unhappy about the smelly boatyard and the thought of staying the night there. Bob doesn't know that, because he's paying attention to the boatman, and Zelda is just thinking these things. The only clue that Bob could perhaps really get is that Zelda suddenly says she wants to go. What does that action suggest to him about her attitude?

I think there are two main ways you can read into Zelda's behaviour if you're Bob, and it depends on the kind of "Bob" you're going to be.

For example, if you are Bob and you really wanted to have this boat trip because you want to get away from city life, a bit back to nature, enjoy a new hobby, and all the kinds of expectations we were looking at in A1, but Zelda suddenly seems bored, fed up, and impatient to leave the boatyard where you had been fascinated by the boatman, how would you feel?

Probably equally fed up and annoyed. Zelda isn't "getting into the spirit" of it. She doesn't even seem to be *trying* to get into the spirit of it. She's letting you know that this was NOT her idea of a holiday, and she's probably trying to ruin it for you.

If you were Bob, you'd feel just like any real person who is enthusiastic about something but who can't get your friend, your bae, or your parents to be keen about your hobby.

(Have you ever seen "Despicable Me"? Remember when Gru keeps trying to get his mother to acknowledge his brilliant inventions, and all she says is, "Meh"? That response is really unsupportive, hurtful, and disheartening, isn't it?)

In this Bob persona, you could write to your brother something like: "I just really didn't understand Zelda's attitude. Here we were, getting all this great information from the boatman about lingo and the area, and all she wanted to do was leave. I found it really frustrating."

That's Bob Mach 1.

What if, however, you were hen-pecked Bob. We'll call him Bob Mach 2. You feel guilty about bringing Zelda on the trip. You know she likes glitz and shopping and the theatre, but you kind of hoped she'd enjoy herself once she got into the great outdoors. But now you see you were wrong. You feel BAD! You want to be apologetic about the whole thing, and perhaps a bit of a limp dishrag about it.

DO: Rewrite my answer above as an apologetic Bob, justifying Zelda's behaviour rather than being annoyed by it. Don't forget to express your feelings about her actions. A possible answer can be found at the back of the book.[4]

DO NOT PROCEED
Without doing the task first

- *Important Tip: Note that the bullet point says write about YOUR FEELINGS (as Bob) about Zelda's behaviour. Don't just list what Zelda's behaviour was. There were a lot of students who struggled with the nuance of the question because they didn't read it carefully! (Memory Verse!!!!)*

A3

Finally, let's look at the third bullet point, A3. In this section, you are to *make up* or *create* things that you and Zelda did on the rest of the trip that aren't mentioned in Passage A.

However, don't think you can list a bunch of random things that aren't prepared for in the passage. For example, you won't gain many points for saying you went bowling, sky-diving, or even gardening. You need to look carefully at the passage and at ideas that were *planted* in it — natural progressions from what is already there.

Remember when I said earlier that Bob's expectations might include socialising with other boaters? Why not have them meet up with some other boaters?

DO: Look carefully at Passage A and find some other people they could meet up with or do something with as an example of what they did on the rest of their trip. Circle the reference to them in the passage, and then jot down what Bob and Zelda did with them in your notebook.

LESSON TWO

DO NOT PROCEED
Without doing the task first

At the back of the book, you'll see some of the people whom I think Bob and Zelda could have done something with; but of course, meeting people is just one activity that's planted in Passage A.[5]

- Can you find something about another restaurant to visit?
- Can you find something about a historical place to visit?
- Can you find something about nature study they could have done?

How do you think Zelda feels about these different activities? It's up to you to decide if she ever gets in the swing of things, if she continues to be a grump, or if, after all that trouble, Bob ends up calling off the whole trip and going home early.

General Point about Question 1

I hope you're getting the idea that reading the passage is sort of like a hunt for clues. Sure, there are easy surface answers for the having, but anyone can find those. If it's easy enough that anyone can find them, you know they're not going to be useful for separating great answers from the MEHHHH ones.

So don't just read: read SMART!

Variations of Question 1

Be aware that this question is only one type of question you might get.

This one, for example, is based on a passage with two characters, one of which is a viewpoint character. It's Zelda's version of the situation first, and you have to alter this viewpoint to be Bob's instead, and write his view in a different genre.

A very similar exam can be found in June 2016 Paper 21, where we get a hotelier's view of a couple's visit as the insert material, and the task is to write a letter from the wife's point of view about her husband.

So while this approach on Question 1 is fairly typical, there are others that might crop up.

Another version you can get is a single person's specific story, where you are asked to make use of that specific information and generalise it, usually to a different audience in a different genre. A story about someone's first horseback riding experience, say, might be turned into a speech about how one might ride a horse for the first time. Or, as seen in 2019's sample paper, a first sky-diving experience might be translated into a speech to first-time sky-divers from an instructor's view.

You can also get a story where the main character has to write a journal entry about what happened in the story, as seen in 0500-22 June 2017; or where the character is interviewed by somebody. This latter type could be a manager asking what went wrong, or someone on the radio asking questions. An example can be seen in 0500-23 Winter 2016.

The Bigger Point

In other words, practising past papers a lot is a good idea to see the different variations of this question, but it will never prepare you for every option that might come up. That's why you need to be good at the SKILLS they're testing here:

- Can you read and understand what Passage A means on the surface?
- Can you read between the lines and infer information?
- Can you adopt a different viewpoint from the one in the passage?
- Can you alter the genre of passage to one with a different audience, style, and purpose?

* * *

- *Important Tip: Online, scripts are marked for three levels of reading for Question 1:*

    - *The straightforward point — say, for example, that Bob expected to treat Zelda with a canal boat holiday. Because this observation belongs to the first bullet point of the question, it would be labeled with an "A1". If, on the other hand, you were referring to the third bullet point, that Bob and Zelda met the celebrity couple and had drinks on their boat, then that would be noted by "A3". The more A1, A2, and A3 you have, the higher your mark is likely to be.*
    - *Next comes the detail from the passage — Bob wanted "peace and quiet". These get tick marks to show you referred to the insert. The more of these details you include, the higher your mark is likely to be.*
    - *Finally, the development (DEV)... this is the "because" statement. For example, Bob expected to have some peace and quiet on the holiday because they could get a change of scenery from the city, where it's implied they live.*

Reading Ability is Important, but Writing Ability Counts Too!

There are five marks available for your writing on this question. This includes:

- being able to use your own words and consider the audience appropriately
- good sentence structures and variation
- wide variety of vocabulary, accurate spelling, competent punctuation
- organising your answer (using the bullet points as given in the question is the best idea)

BUT IT IS ONLY 5 POINTS!

In other words, don't sweat the details of the genre.

Yes, write a letter that starts: "Dear Brian, We've just come back from a trip I arranged for Zelda as a surprise …" because that's what you've been told to do on the exam paper. However, it isn't helpful for your mark to expand this letter into too much chit-chat about your brother's life, his family, the swimming competitions they're doing, etc. You're not being asked to write a REAL letter. It's an exam answer – a CONSTRUCT to help you show off how well you can pick out information, read between the lines, and develop your answer in good writing skills.

In Lesson Two, you've learned:

- Question 1 wants you to read Passage A and change the kind of writing it is and/or its viewpoint.
- Question 1 gives you a starting point that you should use, and three bullet points that you should follow.
- The more relevant points you find, the more details you include, and the more development you do, the better your mark is likely to be.
- There are also 5 points for writing that includes a lot of different skills.
- Remember that this is an exam answer that mainly shows off your reading ability, and doesn't really want you to "get into" the genre of the assignment so much that you forget to focus on the details of Passage A.

Revision Suggestions from Lesson Two: Genres

Review different kinds of writing

Here's a cheeky tip for getting a quick review of writing conventions for different styles you might see on the exam. These are older versions of the Collins exam guide, and they are still searchable on Amazon. The covers may vary (as of this writing, there isn't ANY cover picture), but the link still works.

When using "look inside," choose the table of contents and click on any of the underlined headings in Chapter 3: Key Writing

Skills. You'll see a lot of content that you can read and learn from.

You could even use "Print Screen" on your computer to capture the screen image and print it out for studying.

https://tinyurl.com/y94nray9

Final assignment for Lesson Two

DO: Try your hand at doing Question 1 on your own, following the tips and suggestions in this lesson. Then, compare your answers to the mark scheme that's available here: https://tinyurl.com/y8qmp6az. How many of their expected points did you find?

Lesson Three

In this lesson, we're going to turn our attention to Question 2 on the "Reading" paper, or 0500-21/22/23. We will be referring to the June 0500-22 paper, so you need to have it in front of you during this lesson.

First, let's review what we did in Lesson Two.

- We looked at the advantage of using marginal markers on Passage A for calming down, for getting your facts right, and for making your comprehension stronger.
- We looked at Question 1 and thought about general principles:

    - Know your material before you start writing (narrate to solidify details).
    - Know the style of writing required (report, letter, speech, interview, etc.).

LESSON THREE

>   - Read the question carefully so you know what's important (make use of any bullet-point guidance).
>   - Don't lose sight of the point of the answer (which is to show that you have read carefully and accurately).

- We looked at the specifics of Question 1 on the 0500-22 from June 2015, and discovered that it wanted an answer in three parts, written as a friendly letter to a brother.
- We looked at how an answer like this is marked: addressing the bullet points (A1, A2, A3), detail from the passage, and development ("because").
- For revision tips, you were encouraged to look at a book available to search on Amazon that can help you learn more about different styles of writing, such as letters.

0500-21/22/23 Question Two at a Glance

This question is all about language analysis. In my opinion, a big percentage of the scripts I mark are rubbish at doing this. I am going to reveal to you the formula you can use to not only answer this question well, answer it easily, and answer it thoroughly, but which I also believe will teach you how to analyse literature effectively in general. Above all, it will help you finally understand what literature is all about.

First, let's establish what Question 2 wants:

- Can you choose words or phrases that add to the passage's meaning?
- Can you understand the basic meaning of the phrase you've chosen?
- Can you see how the author has used language to achieve certain effects?

Therefore, you need to:

1. make good choices
2. explain the basic meaning (narration!)
3. explain how the author achieves effects.

The other important part of Question 2 to establish right now is that it's worth only 10 points. Those points are entirely interested in how well you can read what the passage is saying; in other words, how the author adds extra "atmosphere" or "personality" through the words and phrases he/she chooses.

The question does NOT mark your writing skill, and for that reason, I will show you a format for writing your answers that will help you get the maximum reading points without wasting time on an essay-like format.

But first, let's talk about how to analyse the effects that the author is creating so you have something to say that gets credit.

To me, effective language analysis is like peeling back the layers of an onion

I've created a five-step approach that I have called the HOW hand for helping you peel these layers in a focused and effective way.

I've called it the HOW hand because I use all five fingers of your hand to help you remember the five important steps. When you hold your hand with the palm out, as in a greeting to someone, it reminds me of the way that native Americans were stereotypically said to greet the white man in old cowboy films — hand palm out, saying, "How!"

Edward S Curtis, 1906

In list form, this is how your five stages look:

- Pick a good phrase or word
- Pick ONLY a phrase or word; not a long sentence
- Explain what it means in plain terms (the outer-most layer, or "just the facts, Ma'am")
- Explain what else it can mean, or what it can suggest, or what it might imply (a deeper layer of meaning)
- Explain HOW the writer achieves effects by using this language

In visual form, it's like this:

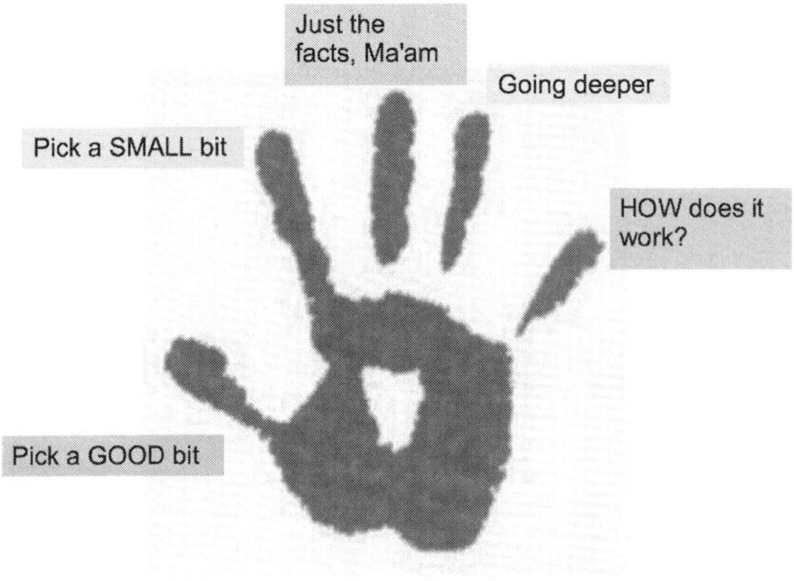
Just the facts, Ma'am
Going deeper
Pick a SMALL bit
HOW does it work?
Pick a GOOD bit

It's important to note that your thumb and forefinger are about good choices — a crucial stage of this question. If you hold up just your thumb, it's like saying "good". If you hold your thumb and forefinger like a pretend gun-shape, then hopefully you can think of this stage as pointing at a target. You want to hit the bulls-eye. Sometimes, students think I mean to choose just ONE word. In reality, you need to choose the words or phrases that complete the idea, but only ONE idea.

An old exam used to talk about how a bunny "pranced" and "twirled," and some people would choose both of those words in a single phrase. But think about it: those are different images of how the bunny moves, so they are two different choices. On the other hand, if a candidate chose only "leaps" instead of "rehearsing its leaps" for that bunny, they wouldn't get the same idea of the bunny's performance with that word "rehearsing." Sometimes, a single word is okay; sometimes you need a phrase. Really reading the context of the language will help you choose which is right.

The other three fingers are the steps toward deepening the layers of your explanation. You need to start off with something I call "just the facts, ma'am." The phrase comes from an old detective show where one of the cops would always interrupt a witness who told too long a story. He only wanted the facts. The straightforward answer.

This straightforward answer is actually one of the two things the question is looking for. Do you understand the straightforward meaning of this phrase as it appears in the story? The other thing it's looking for is whether you can explain what kind of "quality" is added by the specific choices of the author.

For example, if I were to talk about a car whose back seat felt like a bed of nails, I wouldn't want you to tell me it's a simile that makes the words stand out. That doesn't tell me either the meaning or the effect.

Instead, look at the straightforward meaning first, or "just the facts, ma'am." It should be fairly obvious that the simile is just another way of saying that the car's back seat is really uncomfortable. That's what "like a bed of nails" means in plain terms.

To get to the second part of what the examiner is looking for, you often need to take a couple of steps – the kind of logical progression from how "bed of nails" brings to mind torture; or perhaps extreme, almost guru-like hardship.

To get there, I take an intermediate step which I call "going further." I've already said that the phrase means the back seat is uncomfortable, but "bed of nails" is more than just uncomfortable, right? I mean, the author could have said it was hard as a rock or stiff as a plank, and these similes have their own images pop up in our heads if we think about it.

Somehow, we have to get from the fact that the back seat is uncomfortable to how the "bed of nails" indicates that. We look, then, at "bed of nails." What is a bed of nails? Clearly, it's not a comfy bed, but one made of metal spikes. Therefore, the back seat of the car is uncomfortable and reminds the young boy of a kind of torturous, spikey bed.

Finally, we put it all together – the back seat of the car is so uncomfortable that it reminds the boy of a bed made of metal spikes; a phrase that shows either that the car isn't really suitable for its purpose, or that the boy is a grump and complains, exaggeratedly, about his experience.

I have just taken you through the five steps of the HOW hand with one example, and now I'm going to do it again with a different example.

Let's try the HOW hand with an example from an old exam

Below, I have copied a passage from "Honey Hotel," the June 2016 exam.

In this extract, the hotelier is going through the submissions to his travel-writing contest, and his wife shows him one that she thinks is best:

> He agreed. Reading the winning entry, he'd been entranced by the sensitivity with which its gifted writer staged scenes of ancient civilisations and romantic journeys along half-forgotten sandy roads – conjuring a charming mirage of white-washed walls, embroidered gowns and orange trees laced with sunlight.

Normally in an exam, you have more context for the passage than I've just provided here, because you will have to read the whole passage from the insert. Even so, the technique will be the same — pick out words and phrases that add meaning to the passage.

What do I mean by that? Basically, just choose words or phrases that add pictures, imagery, and/or extra atmosphere to the passage.

Remember that analysing language for Question 2 is a) about good choices, b) about telling both meaning and effect, and c) thinking around the phrase so you don't analyse in isolation and say something that shows you didn't read very carefully after all!

DO: Look at the passage above: do you see any words or phrases that stick out as especially literary or notable? Look first for similes or metaphors, but if there aren't any, look for "imagery" – words that create pictures in your head. Jot them down in your notebook before I tell you a couple I've picked out as possibilities.

DO NOT PROCEED
Without doing the task first

Here are some of the options that I noted. These are the possibilities stated in the mark scheme, and note: ONLY the choices in the mark scheme will get points! I'll re-visit this in a minute.

He agreed. Reading the winning entry, he'd been entranced by the sensitivity with which its gifted writer staged scenes of ancient civilisations and romantic journeys along half-forgotten sandy roads – conjuring a charming mirage of white-washed walls, embroidered gowns and orange trees laced with sunlight.

How'd you do? Did you find any of the same phrases? Give yourself a big red "A" on your notebook if you got at least two of these! Hooray!

Now I'm going to take one of these examples and show you how to write it for the CIE exam, using a model that will save you time and get you maximum points.

I'm going to choose the one about "orange trees laced with sunlight."

On the surface, this just means that there are trees that produce oranges (this may have needed you to read carefully – sometimes, students think the trees are actually orange in colour, but the context of the passage shows they're in a kind of Spain-like location, so you should be able to work out that they're fruit trees — they are not orange-coloured a la sunset or autumn)

The first thing I do is think through my steps of the HOW hand – my good bit/small bit is "orange trees laced with sunlight." Then I think of how to explain the straightforward meaning of it. What does it say … just the obvious?

It says that the orange trees are being lit up by the sun.

PLEASE DON'T FORGET THIS STEP!!!! If you forget the "just the facts, ma'am" step, you will miss out on something the examiner is looking for. You may even start analysing down the wrong path, having not established the right one to use.

Next is "going further." Are there special qualities, pictures, or extra atmosphere added by this choice of words? Here, it's that the sun's light is "laced." Sometimes, I think about alternatives that could be used, like burnt or cloaked or blanketed with sunlight instead of laced, and that can help direct my thoughts toward which quality the author is trying to achieve.

Here, "laced" is clearly a kind of dappled or gentle effect, because lacy clothing is soft and see-through, and would create a gentleness to the sunlight.

Putting it together, I'll sum it all up in HOW the phrase is working in the passage: the author seems to be creating a quality of sunlight that's gentle and beautiful — perhaps even feminine, since lace is often seen on women's clothing.

Having now gone through the five steps of the HOW hand, here's how to write out the answer:

"orange trees laced with sunlight"

The sun filtering through the fruit trees is giving off dappled light. Dappled light isn't a harsh light, so it's not too hot or glaring, as is emphasized by the use of the word "laced" – the sun's light is made to seem more fragile or precious, and perhaps even feminine because of the connection with lacy clothing.

DO: Using five different-coloured pens or pencils, underline the parts in "Here's how to write out your answer" above that correspond to

- Good bit

- Small bit

- Just the facts, ma'am

- Going deeper

- HOW does it work?

Yes, the first two are the same phrase, but I still want you to underline it in two different colours so you come to understand that they're each important, even though (when you get it right) they refer to the same choice of text.

DO NOT PROCEED
Without doing the task first

Summary About Question 2

Analysing language is a) about good choices, b) about telling both meaning and effect, and c) thinking around the phrase so you don't analyse in isolation and say something that shows you didn't read very carefully after all!

Question 2 from 0500-22

Now it's time to refer to your question paper and get some practice at the HOW hand for yourself. The instructions on the exam for Question 2 will tell you which two paragraphs you're to focus on; it's no good picking out interesting words and phrases from any part of Passage A other than the one the exam tells you to look at (remember your memory verse???).

In this case, your task is to look at two specific paragraphs and:

- find "powerful" words and phrases from each of these paragraphs (that would be the "good bit" from our HOW hand);
- include imagery (in other words, word pictures);
- explain HOW the choice is used effectively.

Let's start with Paragraph 6 from the insert, which starts: "No sooner were we inside." The task says to look at words and phrases about the storm and its effects.

DO: Read through Paragraph 6 and pick a good bit/small bit. Start by choosing the obvious and easy phrases first, such as similes. Once you have picked the obvious literary simile, write out your "just the facts, ma'am," where you tell back in plain terms exactly what that phrase is talking about in the context of the story.

LESSON THREE

DO NOT PROCEED
Without doing the task first

The only simile in this paragraph is the one in the first sentence: "like machine gun fire." If you were to write the "just the facts, ma'am" of JUST this little phrase, you might say something like, "it sounded like a machine gun going off." However, you need a bit more than this to properly explain what that simile means — WHAT sounds like machine gun fire? The rain! More specifically, Zelda thought the rain from the storm sounded like machine gun fire as it pelted the roof of the boat.

BUT WAIT!!!! It's really important that you put "just the facts, ma'am" into your own words. The reason is this: many students who are not native English speakers or who are not very strong in English will simply parrot back a phrase when they don't really understand what it means. Therefore, the mark scheme is very clear in expecting that good answers will not "repeat the language of the original."

Instead, try something like this:

> "The rain on the canal boat's roof sounded like the rapid, heavy pattering of shots from an automatic gun."

(Note: Occasionally, you might feel the need to undertake massive verbal gymnastics in order to avoid the original language. If you think it's getting a bit silly — I mean, how else can you say "dog" unless you twist yourself into all kinds of unnecessary knots? — then it's probably okay to use the original word. Just make sure that you include enough detail so that the examiner can tell you really understand what you're talking about.)

Next, Step Four in the HOW hand wants you to "go further." This step is in here so you don't leap straight into literary labelling, and thus don't explain how your thought processes got you there.

This is just like my earlier example of the lacy sunlight. You don't just say the orange trees were being lit up by the sun and it was gentle — that would mean skipping the bit where you explained about lace.

In the exam's Passage A, the good bit/small bit is taking the topic of rain and relating it to an instrument of warfare.

DO: Think about the connection between rain and machine guns. Describe in your own words what machine-gun rain would sound like, and the kind of feeling it's creating for the scene. Check my suggestions below once you've jotted down your thoughts.

LESSON THREE

DO NOT PROCEED
Without doing the task first

So far, you have chosen a good bit/small bit. You have written a sentence of "just the facts, ma'am." Now, you have added the going further, explaining the transition of rain into something loud, rapid, and probably quite violent or aggressive.

What do you think the author is trying to tell us about this rain storm by making this simile? Clearly, it's not meant to be your usual pitter-patter experience! No comparisons to playful kittens, in other words!

To help you, we're going to play a multiple choice quiz. From the following options, which "HOW" explanation is closest to what the simile is doing here?

A. By comparing the rain to a machine gun, the author is making it all stand out.

B. By comparing the rain to a machine gun, the author is talking about how loud the rain is.

C. By comparing the rain to a machine gun, the author is suggesting that this is an aggressive and violent storm.

D. By comparing the rain to a machine gun, the author uses a simile that describes the storm.

Hopefully, you chose the right answer. You can check at the back of the book.[6]

DO: Now write out your answer to "like machine gun fire" in the same format that I wrote about the orange trees being laced like sunlight. As always, you can find a possible answer at the back of the book.[7]

DO NOT PROCEED
Without doing the task first

About Overview

One final touch you can put on your responses to Question 2 is that of "overview," where you consider several of these good bit/small bit answers as a group, or look at the paragraph as a whole.

For example, if you look back over Paragraph 6, what would you say is the overall feeling of the weather? Even just a glance at some of the key words — hammering, shrieking, snatched — points to a rather frightening, noisy, and powerful storm.

DO: Now, re-read Paragraph 7, that begins "Having only managed ..." What is the overall feeling of this paragraph? What are some of the key words that made you say this?[8]

DO NOT PROCEED
Without doing the task first

- *Important Tip: Choices on Question 2 are really key. The mark scheme dictates which choices are considered acceptable. In other words, if you thought a good bit from Paragraph 6 was "the wind rose," or "the boat pitched at its mooring," then you would be out of luck. They don't appear on the mark scheme, and you would actually be penalised for making poor choices. Lots and lots of practice with old papers will get you thinking like the mark scheme!*

In Lesson Three, you've learned:

- Make sure you know which paragraphs you are to take words and phrases from in Passage A.
- Make sure you pick out words/phrases that have layers of meaning. Anything with obvious literary techniques,

such as metaphors, personification, or imagery, are good to choose. It shows you understand how these techniques work.

- Don't quote too long a section; stick with a few words at the most. Otherwise, you don't get credit for more than one accepted item in the phrase.
- Choose quality over quantity in terms of how many phrases you write about – the minimum should be 3 from each paragraph if you write the length of my example, plus some overview if you have time.
- Use your HOW hand to write a complete answer – the outer layer, the inner layer, and the techniques used. Don't just label; explain!

Revision Suggestions from Lesson Two: Genres

Review Literary Terms

It's really important for Question 2 that you know literary terms and how they work. Otherwise, you haven't got the knowledge to know what makes a good phrase, and you haven't got the vocabulary or understanding to explain HOW the author achieves effects with that phrase.

Since these are the two objectives being examined in Question 2, you need to know literary terms!

There are several pages of literary terms with brief explanations of HOW they work at this BBC Bitesize link: http://www.bbc.co.uk/education/guides/zs9gtyc/revision

However, there's no need to go "overboard" with all the different techniques; those on their first page will probably do (simile, metaphor, onomatopoeia, alliteration, and personification).

Final assignment for Lesson Three

DO: Find as many past papers as you can for Paper 2 and print off their Passage A, their question 2 from the question paper, and their mark scheme for question 2. Remember that this question hasn't changed for years — you can easily go back 5 years or more, and print off all three versions of both Winter and Summer exams. Then, with a partner or a parent, see how many of the good bit/small bit choices you can make that are included as official answers in the mark scheme.

Lesson Four

In this lesson, we're going to turn our attention to Question 3 on the "Reading" paper, or 0500-21/22/23. We will be referring to the June 0500-22 paper, so you need to have it in front of you during this lesson.

First, let's review what we did in Lesson Three.

- We were exposed to the HOW hand and its five steps to successful literary analysis.
- We looked at Question 2, and saw that it wanted to find out:

    1. Can you choose words or phrases that create deeper meaning?
    2. Can you understand the basic meaning of the phrase you've chosen?
    3. Can you see how the author has used

language to achieve certain effects?

- For revision tips, you were encouraged to look at some online resources for strengthening your knowledge of literary terms.

0500-21/22/23 Question Three at a Glance

The one about pinpoint comprehension, written in a short, succinct paragraph.

Now, I know that I am using a paper from the old "spec" that still has 3a and 3b, but my reason for doing this is to help you use the 3a stage to write your answer for the new kind of exam. The list still has to be made; it just doesn't have to be written on the answer booklet anymore.

Question 3 now comes in only one part, and your answer has a limit of 250 words. It receives 15 points for your reading ability (i.e. the old list of 15 points, although there is now greater emphasis on implicit as well as explicit meaning, and on grouping ideas), and 5 marks for how well you write in terms of concision. That's a total of 20 points — the same as in the old paper.

It should be an easy question — just read a passage, note down as many relevant points as you can find, organise them effectively, and write them in continuous prose. However, you can get yourself in a big muddle with it if you …

… don't read the question!

This is one reason that I have you copy down that memory verse every day as part of your revision. Honestly, if you can't read the question properly, then how can you give the correct answer? It's just logic.

Here are some tips for approaching Question 3 in a systematic and focused way:

- Make sure you read the question.
- With the task in mind, first go through the passage and underline points that you think are relevant.
- Briefly evaluate the points in light of the question – are any of them saying the same thing in two ways (e.g. hares have longer ears; rabbits have shorter ears).
- Try to re-arrange the ideas from the passage into topics that go together; this is what is meant by "overview" in

Band 1 of the mark scheme, and is more effective than just writing down the ideas in the order they appear in the passage.
- Once you have gathered your points and grouped them, just start writing your answer. The new mark scheme doesn't clarify whether or not intros and conclusions will be penalized like they have been for many years prior to this, but since it's looking for "concision," then it still seems to be the right advice to jump straight into the answer without them.
- Speaking of concision, the question stipulates that your answer should be 250 words or less. This is a new limit, and I suspect it's very important to keep within the word count if you want a good grade.

Finally, a word of warning – examiners aren't allowed to fill in a candidate's gaps, so you have to write clearly about what you mean. If you were just to say, using the example above, that hares and rabbits have different-sized ears, then it's not likely that you'll get credit for that answer. It wasn't clear or accurate enough.

Question 3a from 0500-22

Remember that your exam isn't going to have a 3a, but let's just use it for seeing the question and jotting down notes for things that will go in your new Question 3.

First, let's look at the instructions from the question paper.

Ignore the ones about notes and writing in your own words – look at the question. It's about "challenges faced during the construction" of the Panama Canal. Note that it's NOT asking about the history of the canal, how the canal works, or details about (for example) the lake along the way.

Finally, just before you start reading Passage B and finding answers in it, locate the italicised description of what Passage B is about. Underline it to give you context for the piece you're about to read.

Answering strategy:

Read a sentence at a time from Passage B. After each sentence, ask yourself: is this about the challenges faced when constructing the canal? If it isn't, just move on.

DO: Using a pen or pencil, go through the first three paragraphs of Passage B and underline phrases that mention problems that were faced when building the canal.[9]

DO NOT PROCEED
Without doing the task first

- *Important Tip: There are two issues to keep in the back of your mind as you pick out the relevant phrases you want to write in your 250 words.*

  1. *First, combining similar issues. Some of the answers are different ways of saying the same thing. For example, you might be tempted to write that it was costly, a company went bankrupt, and an American company spent $387 million, thinking that these were worth three points. In reality, all three points are grouped under the subject of expense. It's okay to gather up these three points and write them together in a sentence, but you're likely to get just one point out of it.*
  2. *Second, separating similar issues. In some exams, I have seen examples of general points that SHOULD be separated. I'm thinking of the bunny paper again. It's entirely appropriate to write about how hares are a) independent when they're born, and b) born with their eyes open. These are separate points on the mark scheme. Putting these two points in a single sentence, along with other points in the passage about young hares, is a good example of the sort of concision and overview that this question is looking for.*

With these tips in mind, go back over your third paragraph and see if there are any challenges for the canal that could be combined. I'll do one to start with: malaria and yellow fever would be part of the same problem, which might be said to be health risks or diseases. If I were to answer this question, I could put malaria and yellow fever in the same sentence when talking about health risks, but I would receive one mark for the two phrases.

It's okay to do this if you have plenty to discuss, because giving examples is a stronger way of showing you know what you're talking about. It's probably better than just writing "health risks" by itself.

DO: Circle two points in the third paragraph that are connected with difficult terrain or problems with the geography of the area.[10]

DO NOT PROCEED
Without doing the task first

LESSON FOUR 55

More Revision Practice Ideas

Although this is a new format for 0500 this year, you can still benefit from looking through Question 3s from past papers. Learning to pick out what points are relevant, and also how to combine or separate them, would be useful revision. The papacambridge.com site has a lot of mark schemes to help you with this.

Another reason to practise old papers is to get more chances at reading the question. I can't stress enough how many mistakes are made on Question 3 because a candidate didn't read the focus of the question carefully enough.

After the pre-writing stage

Now that you have identified a good number of points from the passage — some of which you have combined, all of which you have grouped — it's now time to turn them into a flowing passage of prose that you'll write in your own words.

The key word for this answer is:

condensed

That says "Dense," meaning that you need to write in a very focused way.

Taking the seven points that we found in the third paragraph of the insert and jotted down as notes, let's look at how I'd turn this into a dense summary for Question 3.

"Some of the challenges faced by building the canal were engineering problems, bad living conditions for the workers, and difficulty in managing the project. There were a lot of illnesses, like malaria, because of the area. Mosquitos were contributing to these health issues, so the builders required actions like spraying and draining the swamps. The land caused issues, too — too much rain caused the mud to collapse back into the excavations. These obstacles all mounted up in terms of the high cost of the project."

NOTICE that "Some of the challenges faced by building the canal" is as much introduction as you need for this answer. You would go on in this vein with the rest of your eight points, making sure that you stay focused, use your own words within reason, and aim for fluency. Watch your spelling and grammar, too!

Remember that all this has to be done in less than 250 words. By the way, my example above was 87 words long.

There is one catch, though.

LESSON FOUR

We're not looking — maybe the catch will go away!

The catch is that your fifteen choices from the pre-writing stage have to be good, or your answer for Question 3 won't be concise, dense, and accurate.

Question 3 is looking for:

- Using your own words
- Writing fluently
- Packing in the relevant points from the passage so that the summary is concise
- Avoiding introductions, conclusions, or unnecessarily long explanations
- *Important Tip: There are two additional "boosts" to your answer that are available to you. The first is nice writing — good vocabulary, strong sentences. The second is organising your answer, especially grouping ideas that were spread out in Passage B. Remember the grouping of ideas in your pre-*

writing stage, where I mentioned that yellow fever and malaria were actually one point about health dangers. Since these were dangers to people, you could group other topics together in one paragraph, such as diseases, housing, draining swamps, netting, and high death toll. This is what the mark scheme is getting at when it talks about "overview."

Here's a Crazy Idea!

What if you actually START on Question 3 in the exam? You could decide to use only half an hour on it to grab a good dozen marks before turning your attention to Questions 1 and 2.

Believe it or not, there's even an argument for doing the whole question backwards. Think about it — Question 1 is the trickiest in terms of taking time over it, and you might gain insight for Question 1 by doing Question 2 first. I mean, did you notice how Zelda's attitude on the morning after the storm was starting to soften toward her surroundings — how she began to find the scenery inviting, quiet, and precious? Knowing that before writing Question 1 could have a big effect on the A3 section of your answer!

If you do decide to tackle the paper backward, you must start doing this on all your mocks and practices!

In Lesson Four, you've learned:

- Make sure you have read and understood the question (memory verse!).
- Take notes just like the old 3a, combine together those of the same topic, and group your ideas so you can write a structured, concise summary.
- Your answer is likely to be stronger if you:

    - don't write an intro or conclusion
    - don't waffle and explain too much, but just churn out those points you identified

- Consider starting with Question 3.

Revision Suggestions from Lesson Four: Expose Yourself

Explore a wide variety of genres

What I mean by "expose yourself" has nothing to do with macks and a lack of underwear! Instead, I mean it's time to intentionally gather, read, and study the kinds of writing that you might have to produce in your 0500 exams.

What kinds of writing might you have to do? According to CIE's spec, you could have to write:

- a report
- a letter
- a journal entry (like a diary)
- a speech
- an interview
- a newspaper report
- a magazine article

You will also be reading inserts in your exams that may be taken from similar kinds of writing, so the more "exposure" you have to a variety of written materials, the better.

Start by picking up a variety of papers and magazines from newsagents. Look up Martin Luther King Jr's "I have a dream" speech, or Sojourner Truth's "Ain't I a woman" speech. Google some non-fiction news reports, look up some extracts from Anne Frank's diary or other famous diary writers, find radio transcripts or interviews ... I think you get the drift, right?

DO: Copy the bullet-point list above and cross out each one as you deliberately revise the different kinds of writing.

Finally, add another 5 minutes to your copywork every day, where you copy from an example from your "exposure" texts as well as your literary text.

All this being said, remember that genre conventions are only a tiny portion of your mark – and really only impression-marking at that. It's much more important to be able to understand the passages from the exam, so while you're "exposing yourself" to all these different genres, it is equally important to narrate all of them to practise your comprehension.

Don't forget to challenge yourself sometimes with harder examples!

Final assignment for Lesson Four

DO: To help you get to grips with Question 3, use the stage that's known as 3a from the past paper we're using here to make notes and prepare to write your summary. Make sure you write it by hand, unless you know you have permission to use a computer in the exam. After you've written your summary, take a brightly-coloured marker and put a big tick on top of each of the points you've made from the mark scheme. Are there lots of them, clumped together? Good. Did you write between 200 and 250 words? Good. If not, you need to get within those parameters. The last self-check stage is to let someone like your parent read the summary out loud and narrate back to you what they think you mean. The reason you do this is that sometimes you've been too general, and what you write doesn't actually reflect the passage fully. Only by getting a fresh eye will you learn when you make this mistake.

Lesson Five

In this lesson, we're going to turn our attention to the Writing Paper, or 0500-31/32/33. We will be referring to the June 0500-31 paper, so you need to have it in front of you during this lesson.

First, let's review what we did in Lesson Four.

- We looked at what Question 3 (in general) is trying to test:

    - Can you pick out a large number of salient points?
    - Can you write them succinctly and densely?

- We used the list of choices in 3a as note-taking before writing the summary needed for the 2019 papers.

- We talked about how it's possible to re-order your approach to Paper 22 if you wanted to start with Question 3.
- The revision tip of the day was about "exposure" — that is, exposing yourself to the types of writing you might have to produce for the exam: articles, reports, diaries, speeches, etc.

0500-31/32/33 in General

- Paper 3 is known as the "writing" paper for the IGCSE, but the first question still receives 10 out of 25 points for assessing your reading!
- Some of the important objectives for this paper are to:

    - order your thoughts
    - demonstrate a range of vocabulary
    - write appropriately for your intended audience
    - show accurate use of mechanics such as grammar, punctuation, etc.

There are two fundamental tasks on this paper:

1. You must have a good grasp of audience and purpose for whichever question you answer.
2. You must aim to write in a fluid, accurate, and orderly manner on all answers.

The Key to the Writing Paper is ... Hats!

Yes, that's right: HATS.

Before you start doing any writing, you need to think through the various kinds of writing styles, tones of voice, purposes, and audiences you're aiming to implement in your answers.

I think it's a bit like looking for a holiday cottage (stay with me — the analogy comes back to hats in a minute). When I look for a cottage, I go onto Google and search "Holiday cottage Britain." This gives me about 50,000 hits for all the holiday cottages in Britain. So I choose an area of the country to focus on, and that eliminates about 45,000 cottages.

Now I have 5,000 to choose from, but I have a big family. And a dog. So I choose various "filters" to narrow my choices more.

By now, I have probably 30 choices — big cottages in the area I want that allow pets. Next filter is the dates I want to travel. Voila! I have successfully limited my choices to one or two, and now I start to contact the rental company and sort out my accommodation.

The hat analogy for the Writing Paper is like this. Rather than filtering out choices on Google as I would do for a holiday home, you are going to figuratively pile hats on your head to achieve the right combination of styles, tones, and purposes for your exam answer. It's a bit like a Venn diagram.

For each question on the paper that you choose to answer, you will "pile" four hats on your head as part of your pre-writing phase. These hats come under the categories:

- Genre hats – what are the conventions for the type of writing? Letters versus speeches versus articles versus essays.
- Audience hats – who are you writing for? Adults, children, friends, strangers, the general public?
- Writer hats – what tone of voice do you want to aim for? (formal, informal, persuasive, angry, descriptive, analytical)

- Purpose hats – why are you writing? To inform, to persuade, to instruct?

Notice that if you circle each of the first initials of these four hats, you get an acronym: GAWP. I know sometimes revision guides talk about only "GAP," but honestly, if you don't think about the attitude and tone you're aiming for as a writer, you can miss the nuances of addressing your answer appropriately.

One way I like to remember this acronym GAWP is to think of someone actually GAWP-ing.

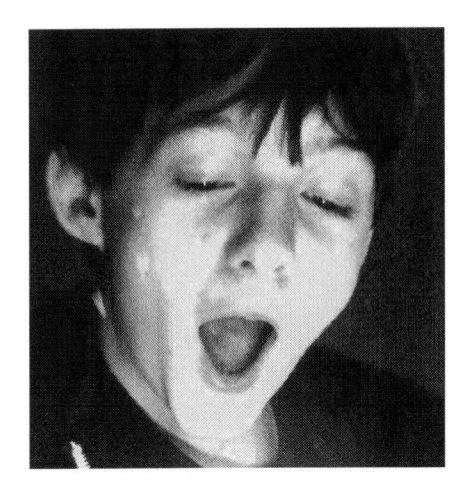

To Gawp: An expression of surprise or alarm
OR
An acronym to help you write better for the exam.

G for Genre

Your genre hats are the ones you choose from to decide the

style of writing. A letter is different from a speech, which is different from a newspaper article, which is different from a journal entry.

A for Audience

After reminding yourself of the conventions for the genre you're supposed to write in, think about who the audience is for the piece. Is it a colleague, a superior officer, a councillor, a teacher, a parent, or a brother? Each of these would require a different approach, so be sure to put on your audience hat before you begin to write.

W for Writer

The oft-overlooked hat. This one makes you think about the persona you're adopting. Are you writing with brotherly affection, the assertiveness of a concerned citizen, the defensiveness of someone who has made a mistake?

P for Purpose

This is no doubt a familiar decision when getting ready to write something — are you doing it to persuade, inform, entertain?

DO: Practise some GAWP-ing right now by jotting down the GAWP of each of these scenarios:

1. A letter to a friend.
2. An interview with your father about his time in the war.
3. A letter of complaint to your local councillor about broken park equipment.
4. A speech to other homeschooled kids about taking up sport.
5. A newspaper article about the closure of a nearby recycling plant.
6. A magazine article about keeping different kinds of pets.
7. A report about the use of swimming pools in your county.
8. A journal entry about being grounded.[11]

A MAJOR PART OF THE 0500-31/32/33 PAPER IS ...

... how well you GAWP!

- Next time, we will look at Question 1 and more GAWP.
- We will also talk about structuring your answers, which is another big part of 0500-31/32/33.
- Plus, in our revision sections, we'll be talking about your writing "mechanics," or proficiency.

REMEMBER that GAWP is really GAWPe (you say this "gawp-ee"). Just like I said about Question 1 on the Reading Paper — where you're supposed to write a letter to your brother, but it's not like any REAL letter you'd write to your brother — you always have to remember that you're writing for an exam.

So one of the hats you always wear is the "e" hat for "exam."

GAWP-e hat

- Next time, we will look more carefully at mechanics,

especially the difference between run-on sentences and sentence fragments.
- Suffice to say, this is a more serious subject than most people realise, and they often fail to give it the attention it needs.
- In this paper, for example, your mechanics make up about one-third of the points for Part 1, and nearly HALF the points for Part 2.
- I have seen many a good writer get limited to the range of "C" for their writing simply because they haven't attended to mechanics.
- This is silly. You should know how to write, punctuate, spell, and manipulate your native language, especially in an exam that's about that very subject!

You still have time to do something about this!

- *Important Tip: Doing copywork routinely will help your spelling, punctuation, grammar, and vocabulary a lot more than any workbook — or even endless correction of your written work — would.*
- *A free grammar workbook focusing on sentences can be found at the following link: https://tinyurl.com/ych3yf3x*
- *It is a challenging 100-page document. I don't mean for you to go through all its exercises, but if you at least read its prose summaries at the beginning of each chapter, you'll get a good overview and some extra help.*
- *I believe you'll get the most out of it if your parents help you*

study it, especially guiding you to focus on those chapters where you have weaknesses.

In Lesson Five, you've learned:

A MAJOR PART OF THE 0500-31/32/33 PAPER IS ...

... how well you GAWP!

- Think of it in terms of hats, piling up the four hats on your head before you start to write.
- Don't forget the fifth hat — "e" — the fact that you're taking an exam!

Revision Suggestions from Lesson Five: Let's Eat Grandpa!*

Mechanics Part A

"Mechanics" refers to your spelling, punctuation, grammar, sentence structures, etc.

Do you know what's wrong with the following sentences and phrases?

> Private:
> Customer Parking
> Only
>
> _____
>
> All others will
> be toad.

> Happy Birthday, Jeanine
> And Underneath that
> We will miss you!

> Irony is when someone texts
> "Your an idiot."
> **********
> Learn grammar; insult properly!

It's important to know correct vocabulary and correct punctuation — it might save a life!

*"Let's eat Grandpa" means that you're planning to dine on your grandad. The writer probably meant to say, "Let's eat, Grandpa," as in, "Come on, Grandpa, let's go get some food."

Here's a link to 15 grammar goofs that make you look silly: http://www.copyblogger.com/grammar-goofs/

And another helpful website for grammar issues:

http://www.bristol.ac.uk/arts/exercises/grammar/grammar_tutorial/index.htm

Final assignment for Lesson Five

DO: Refer to past papers and find at least one example of a journal, an article, an interview, a letter, a report, and a speech. Write down the GAWP of each one, paying particularly close attention to how they differ from each other in the "G" category.

Lesson Six

In this lesson, we're going to turn our attention to Question 1 of 0500-31/32/33. We will be referring to the June 0500-31 paper, so you need to have it in front of you during this lesson.

First, let's review what we did in Lesson Five.

- We saw that, although it's known as the "writing paper," there are still 10 marks out of 25 in Question 1 that assesses your ability to read carefully.
- We saw that this paper is testing various objectives, including:

    - ordering your thoughts
    - demonstrating vocabulary
    - writing appropriately for an audience
    - showing accurate use of mechanics

LESSON SIX

- I told you that there were two fundamental tasks for the Writing Paper, which were:

    - You must have a good grasp of audience and purpose for whichever question you answer.
    - You must aim to write fluidly and accurately on all answers.

- We then went on to look at the different kinds of "hats" that one needs to put on (metaphorically) in order to write appropriately for this exam.

NOTE: choosing hats is also a good way of considering how to appropriately write ANYTHING in real life, too!

- There were four different hats to wear for almost any kind of writing: the acronym I chose for this is GAWP.
- Finally, we looked briefly at the importance of mechanics like grammar and punctuation, and I encouraged you to practise these as much as the techniques of each exam question.

0500-31/32/33 Overview

DO: Look at the cover page of the Question Paper in front of you. Find the paragraph that begins "Answer two questions in the space provided." With a bright-coloured pen or highlighter, underline where it says "two questions." Do the same

for "Question 1 in Section 1, and the ONE question from Section 2." Also underline where it says that you need to clearly write the question number you choose from Section 2 at the start of your answer.

DO NOT PROCEED
Without doing the task first

Note also that there are a total of 50 points for this paper.

You MUST answer Question 1. It's similar to Question 1 of 0500-22 in that you have an insert that you need to read, make marginal markers on, and then re-work the material into a different genre of writing. However, it requires more focus on GAWP than 0500-22 does.

Whereas Question 1 from 0500-22 is marked as 15 points for reading and 5 for writing, Question 1 from 0500-31 is marked as 15 points for writing and 10 points for reading. That's a total of 25 points on the Writing Paper, compared to only 20 points for the Reading Paper.

Then, in Part 2, there is a CHOICE between four questions — 2 choices that are descriptive writing, and 2 choices that are

LESSON SIX 77

narrative writing. You answer ONLY ONE of these, for a total of 25 points.

NOTE — there used to be THREE kinds of writing in Part 2, but since Winter 2014, the option for a discursive essay has been removed. This doesn't mean that past papers prior to June 2015 are useless for revising, but it does mean that they will differ in this regard.

The 25 points for Part 2 of the exam are split into 13 for content and structure, and 12 for style and accuracy.

- "Content and Structure" effectively means the interesting things you write about, and the organisation you put into writing them.
- "Style and Accuracy" means the variety of sentence structures, the wide vocabulary, and your mechanics.

Question 1 from 0500-31

DO: Briefly read through the insert. Write in your notebook what its GAWP is. Now look at Question 1 and write down what GAWP you're supposed to write in for the exam.[12]

DO NOT PROCEED
Without doing the task first

There are several key instructions here:

1. Use the bullet points as topics for each paragraph you write:

> - identify skills and qualities, and evaluate them
> - explain why you want to volunteer, and why you'd be good for the job (Count them, that makes 4 paragraphs!)

2. Use the insert to pull out the answers to these bullet points, making sure you trawl the article for ideas that you can group into your 4 paragraphs.

- *Important Tip: The answer seems to invite you to talk about yourself, but remember that it's really wanting to know how well you have read the article, pulled out relevant points, and organised these into an appropriate piece of writing (This is another example of the "e" in GAWPe).*
- *THIS IS REALLY IMPORTANT — If you find yourself writing a lot about your own ideas and your own experience, you might have misread the focus of the question. There may be some leeway for referencing yourself or your own ideas, but the "e" in GAWPe means that the point will always be more about <u>pulling information</u> out of the insert, <u>evaluating</u> its information, and <u>organising</u> your answer than it will be about your own thoughts.*

DO: Read through the stimulus material. Make your marginal markers. Now, go back through the insert a second

LESSON SIX 79

time while looking for references to qualities and skills for the job, underlining or circling as you go. Finally, pretend like you're getting ready to write Question 3 from 0500-22 and make a list of "salient points" — one list for "qualities" and one list for "skills."

DO NOT PROCEED
Without doing the task first

- *Important Tip: In some past papers, the task has been to evaluate opposing views about something. In that case, you wouldn't make a column of, say, qualities and another for skills. Instead, you would put the pros on one side and the cons on the other.*

Now that you have found a collection of qualities and skills, it will be helpful to go through them and circle those ideas that YOU (or at least, the persona of "you") could bring to this voluntary position. Jot down an example of these qualities or skills.

Finally, the fourth bullet point is about why "you" want to help. There are numerous reasons that you can get from the passage as to why "you" might want to volunteer.

(Why am I putting quotes around "you"? It's to emphasise that this is a construct — the W of GAWP. Hopefully, it will help you maintain a distance between your real life and your persona, so that you stay focused on the insert.)

DO: Write down three reasons why someone would want this job, as implied in the passage.[13]

DO NOT PROCEED
Without doing the task first

One of the ways in which students were coming unstuck on their answers to this question was forgetting the purpose of the position. "You" weren't there to be a super-computer-geek, to impart "your" vast and stupendous knowledge to those who were lucky enough to be in "your" presence!

No, the article states that the job is to "INSPIRE older people about computer technology and help them ENJOY it." The applicant is there in a *service* role, and the actual focus on the job is the elderly person who is there to receive support and encouragement.

It really is important in this question to ensure that you READ

LESSON SIX 81

the insert carefully! The spirit of the insert can often come into play, so be sensitive to it.

Now that you have been through the insert and found the qualities and skills for the job, thought about how "you" fit into those skills, and decided why "you" want to volunteer, you are now ready to write your letter of application.

I'm often asked if it's necessary to include the full address and headings like you would in a real letter, and the simple answer is no. If you follow the instructions and begin your letter, "Dear Age Campaign," and finish off with a Yours Faithfully kind of signature (or Yours Sincerely or Yours Truly or whatever), it will be fairly obvious that you wrote a letter.

It's what you write in between the salutation and the closing that matters!

- *Important Tip: The insert for Paper 3 will often be about something specific, but when you come to write your answer, you often need to generalise these points to fit the GAWPe of the task. Taking the insert of this paper as an example, there is that quote from a specific person — an elderly woman, who is the kind of client that the Age Campaign course is aiming to help. She says that she wishes she could internet shop because she's not as mobile as younger people. This information can be turned into a general point about how elderly people would be greatly helped by learning to buy things on the internet so that they don't need to try to get to the shops anymore. You can then EVALUATE this point or add to it by saying it's a shame that elderly people are being prevented from using such efficient options simply because they don't know how to navigate the internet.*

- *This is really crucial! Input the specifics from the insert, and output generalisations. In fact, some past papers use stimulus material in their inserts that never need referring to in your answer. Obviously, if the Headmaster gives a speech for the insert material, and you're writing a letter to him about his speech, you would reference his speech. However, the insert is sometimes just there to give you information you can include, and you don't even have to refer to the people or situation from the insert in your answer. The raw data is what's important.*
- *For example, several years ago, there was a radio interview of twins about gap years, and the task was to write an article about the pros and cons of gap years. The twins and the radio interview didn't need to feature in the answer at all; simply mining their specifics and turning them into good points, whether pro or con — and evaluating them — was the appropriate use of the insert.*
- *Here's a sample for the start of the letter to Age Campaign:*

"Dear Age Campaign,

My name is Kat Patrick, and I am applying for the position of volunteer in your weekly sessions to help bring the older generation up to date with their technology skills. In an article called "Bridging the Gap," I read that a volunteer doesn't need a great deal of experience with technology — they simply need to have a willingness to connect with the elderly people who are attending the course, and encourage them in their explorations on the computer. I think it's especially important to be more of a listener than a talker, and to find out what aspects of the computer are of most interest to the attendee — whether that's Facebook and other social media, online purchases, Photoshop, or simply being able to send and receive email."

NOTICE HOW:

- *I have focused first and foremost on the general skills needed for this position. I have trawled the insert and pulled out a variety of points, clumping them together in a single paragraph about desirable qualities.*
- *I have used the writer hat. I am being very deferential, focusing on the attendees' wishes rather than my wonderful, stupendous, unsurpassed computer skills that I would wield like a blunt object, bludgeoning my mentee with Twitter and Instagram and all sorts, when the dear little lady might only want to be able to pay her gas bill by direct debit and make a Skype call.*

Finally: More recent past papers have tended to be about pros and cons. In my opinion, that is easier than this paper. While it's very useful to consider pros and cons, the most important skill in Question 1 is evaluation. Using the old gap year question mentioned about the twins, there were plenty of pros and cons for whether a gap year was a good idea or not; but ultimately, you needed to engage your persuasive skills to agree or disagree, and back up your argument with details from the insert.

Some inserts make it easier to find pros and cons than others; these are the ones where the material is more factual. However, an insert will sometimes have an AUTHOR VOICE that the mark scheme wants you to acknowledge, too. For example, if the Headmaster's speech is quite rude towards parents, criticising his rudeness can be part of the answer (as long as you stay respectful). Some other examples from past papers are when a journalist is being sarcastic, or when the author of the insert has some slightly off-base ideas. These are tougher to tackle, so look at plenty of past papers' mark schemes to get an idea of the different kinds of inserts you could come against in your exam.

Above all, take on board this warning. Sometimes, the exam is based on a topic related to school, online learning, or — as is the case for the specimen paper for 2019 — homeschooling. Keep your distance from the topic — "you" is not the same as the real you. Put on your Writer hat of GAWP, focus on the info from the insert only, and avoid talking about your personal beliefs.

In Lesson Six, you've learned:

To write a very good answer for Question 1 according to the

mark scheme, you need to make sure you're doing these four things:

1. Follow the bullet points from the question – usually the first one implies both pros and cons, and the second one wants evaluation. Evaluation is making judgements based on the pros and cons, where you justify your opinion. This is the key distinguisher between a C (an "adequate" answer) and the higher bands.
2. Write in the style that the question asks for.
3. Use the insert to get all your information, going through the material to gather like with like so you don't write your answer in the same order as the material is written in.
4. Make sure that your mechanics are good, including paragraphs.

Revision Suggestions from Lesson Six: Pesky Sentences

Mechanics B

Do you know what makes a good sentence? Do you know the difference between a compound, simple, or complex sentence? More importantly, do you know the difference between a sentence fragment and a run-on sentence?

Maybe you don't know the names of these sentence differences, but you need to know when you've written a complete sentence as opposed to only part of one. You also need to know when you've tried to separate two complete sentences with only a comma.

There is more information about these in the grammar workbook I referred to in Lesson 5, but here's a crash course in sentence structures.

Incomplete sentence, or fragment

An incomplete sentence is one that is missing either a subject or verb — the basic building blocks of a complete sentence. You can have "he ran," but you can't have only "he" or only "ran".

Obviously!

However, most incomplete sentences are longer and more complicated, with lots of words, and yet the subject or the verb is missing.

Example: "Joey, running on empty, flagging at the end of the race."

You might not realise it, but "-ing" words aren't actually verbs. They can be adjectives or parts of verbal phrases when coupled with "was" or "were" and such, but they don't describe a completed action by themselves. You would need to change "flagging" to "flagged" or "was flagging" for the sentence above to be a complete one.

Run-on sentences

Run-on sentences are the opposite of an incomplete one. Often, they are two sentences separated by a comma when stronger punctuation is needed.

Example: "It's half-past five, we can't reach the town after dark now."

In the first sentence, your subject and verb are "It is," and in the second, it's "We can't reach." They are two independent sentences that can't be separated by only a comma.

Correct: "It's half-past five. We can't reach the town after dark now."

or: "It's half-past five, so we can't reach the town after dark now."

or: "It's half-past five; we can't reach the town after dark now."

Only by adding a conjunction (so), or by using a full stop or semi-colon, are the two completed sentences properly separated. You can lose a lot of points for insecure sentence separation.

Final assignment for Lesson Six

DO: Write your own answer for Question 1 about the volunteer job. Be sure to follow the bullet points given, even if it feels forced. Remember not to be crass.

Lesson Seven

In this lesson, we're going to turn our attention to Part 2 of 0500-31/32/33, with a particular focus on Descriptive Writing (usually question numbers 2 and 3). We will be referring to the June 0500-31 paper, so you need to have it in front of you during this lesson.

First, let's review what we did in Lesson Six.

- Last time, we looked at Part 1, Question 1 of Paper 0500-31.
- We looked at four important points about Question 1:

    - Approximate GAWPe while still using the question's instructions re: opening sentence and using the bullet points (in the specific case of the application letter, there were two bullet points with

LESSON SEVEN

      two parts each for a total of 4 paragraphs).
- Make notes where you clump ideas or colour-code details to follow the bullet points in the task, so that you can better organise your answer.
- Input specifics/output generalisations.
- Be sure you evaluate; don't just repeat or agree/disagree without a reason why.
- Pay attention to your mechanics.

- For revision, we explored the difference between run-on sentences and fragments.

Overview of Part 2, 0500-31/32/33

- Part 2 of 0500-31 contains questions 2-5. You answer only ONE of these four choices.

    - 2 and 3 are descriptive writing.
    - 4 and 5 are narrative writing.

- NOTE: In some past papers (prior to 2015), there were three kinds of writing on offer in Part 2. One, the discursive essay, was removed. However, past papers can still be useful when looking at variations of descriptive and narrative writing. Just be aware that they were then numbered 3a/3b and 4a/4b.

- Each question is worth 25 points, split into two parts: Content and Structure (13 points), and Style and Accuracy (12 points).
- The key skill for Content and Structure is making the whole task stick together.
- The key skill for Style and Accuracy is your mechanics and vocabulary.

0500-31/32/33 Part 2, Questions 2 and 3 — Descriptive Writing

There are two key skills in a good description:

1. Envision the scene as a snapshot, so you avoid trying to tell a story when you're supposed to be creating atmosphere; do NOT think like a video, but a photo!
2. Use the analogy of a human body – bones, muscles, and skin – to develop your description to its fullest potential.

Step One: Envision a scene as a snapshot

It's really important to keep your Questions 2 and 3 firmly in the realm of *description,* as in snapshots. Questions 4 and 5 are the *narrative* stories, which are more like video or film, with continuous movement, rising/falling action, etc. It's important not to blur the two!

Let's take a snapshot and describe it in terms of just exactly what's there, without embellishing the details or adding any back story. This is sort of like "just the facts, ma'am" from the HOW hand, but in this case, it's "just the facts, ma'am" about a photograph.

DO: Write down a list of fifteen things you see in this picture.[14]

DO NOT PROCEED
Without doing the task first

This kind of list-taking is what I call the bare bones of a description. It's the basis on which you will build more and more of an overall picture with atmosphere. It's the step you begin with, just like you will start a garden with dirt, seeds, water, and sunlight, but what these create as the plants grow will change the scene enormously.

The only down-side of "bare bones," though, is that they're boring when it comes to a description. Writing an answer like this tends toward just listing details without any specific focus, and gets counted, at best, as Band 4 in the mark scheme as "a series of ordinary details." Band 4 is D-ish.

As I assume you want more than Band 4 — or at least your parents do, or they wouldn't have bought you this book! — then you need to write something more than just a bare-bones description. The exam wants something that connects your description together (muscles), and it wants a texture, an atmosphere in it, like skin on a body.

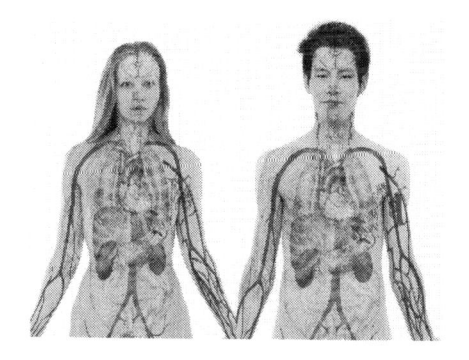

Image from Pixabay

Step Two: Put Muscle on the Bones

For example, here's a detail from the earlier picture with the dog. The barebones of this is "dog."

If I told you simply to picture a dog, you might think of a dalmatian, or a pug, or a cocker-poodle-meranian pinscher. Basically, you and I would really struggle to share the same picture in our heads through simply the word "dog."

So, to convey more detail to you, I might say it's a little black-and-tan terricr with big ears. I might think of the way that its colouring is sort of like Reese's peanut-butter-cup candy. I'm adding detail, but I'm connecting the description by adding extra interest.

Step Three: Adding Skin

Now for what I call the skin, or maybe the "texture" of the description.

See, everyone's got bones. Almost everyone's bones are pretty much the same. I'm sure you've seen the meme where there are seven skeletons, all identical, and underneath each one there's a description of someone's race; the point being made is that everyone is the same underneath, whatever colour their skin, their background, their religion.

On top of bones, almost everyone has muscle, too. Sure, these muscles do different things — a heart muscle doesn't look the same or do the same job as a thigh muscle, but they usually do the same job of connecting things together.

People's skin, however, is usually unique. There are so many different shades, and it can be hairy or smooth, it might have lots of freckles, it might be wrinkly, it will probably have scars, even if it's just from chickenpox!

Think of adding atmosphere to your descriptive writing as though you're describing skin on the muscles. Here's an example:

- The little black-and-tan terrier, the colour of a Reese's

peanut-butter-cup candy, snatched the hat from the boy.
- The little black-and-tan terrier, the colour of a Reese's peanut-butter-cup candy, licked the hat that the boy was holding.
- The little black-and-tan terrier, the colour of a Reese's peanut-butter-cup candy, dodged the boy as he tried to put his hat over her head.

The barebones of the dog, with the muscles of her colour and distinguishing details, and finally, the texture of her movements, all add together to change the atmosphere of the scene.

- **Snatched — rambunctious dog**
- **Licked — playful or sweet dog**
- **Dodged — scared dog**

DO: Look at the following picture and write a bare-bones description of it in your notebook. Use a boring verb to say what it's doing. Label it "bones." Next, try to think of some way to add to its detail, such as describing its colours in

interesting ways. Label this "muscle." Finally, play around with different verbs to add texture or atmosphere to the scene. Label these "skin." Check your answer against my suggestion at the back of the book.[15]

DO NOT PROCEED
Without doing the task first

LESSON SEVEN

It's up to you to take the question's bare bones and turn it into a piece of writing that's full of muscle and skin.

Please note: before writing a single word, think about an overall "body" of writing. In other words, don't add muscle and skin a sentence at a time, but try to come up with an overall atmosphere.

For example, our rambunctious doggy would be better accompanied by giggling children, smiling sunshine, and laughing brooks.

Our licking doggy, on the other hand, could be in a scene where everything is hungry, like caterpillars and butterflies and frogs, etc., so you give an overall view of eating.

A frightened doggy could be in a scene that's tense, with brooding clouds, threatening shadows, aggressive and nasty kids.

- *Important Tip: Description is not simply piling up adjectives. Look at this mish-mash of descriptive words:*

"The rusty old brown door was obstructing my entrance to the gurgling, steamy laboratory that was pitch dark and full of funny smells."

- *This is immature, lazy writing. There is no general feeling of atmosphere, but a hodge-podge of ideas, piled up.[16] Instead, see how this sentence creates an atmosphere of abandonment:*

"An oak door on oxidised hinges led to a laboratory overflowing with broken beakers and seven bunsen burners, each of them dark and disconnected."

Question 2 of Part 2, 0500-31

DO: Look at your exam question paper now for Part 2, subsection Descriptive Writing. We're going to focus on this one for the rest of the lesson, but before we do that, re-write the task in your notebook. What do the instructions say about your beginning point? Note that there's no end point, but finishing off your description at a clear end-point is really important.

DO NOT PROCEED
Without doing the task first

Before you write a single word for your answer, you must — and I mean MUST — stop, look, and listen. This is a tried and true step in the process, so trust me. Make this part of your revision process, pausing to engage your brain before you engage your pen.

- **STOP** panicking and rushing; you need to "breathe in" this scene.
- **LOOK** around your scene – where is this home exactly (suburbs, city centre, countryside)? Is it a brand new house, or only new to you? What are the smells and the sights? Build up a sense of atmosphere.
- **LISTEN** to the house and its surroundings – does it creak and groan, is it solid and silent, does it keep out the noise from the street or do the sounds of a farmyard/a wood/a river invade it, enhance it, involve it?

See if you can get a sense of the kind of house that I'm describing — what is its atmosphere?

"The moment I walked into my new house, I was struck by the colour – brown everywhere. It hadn't been so noticeable before, when the previous owners had their furniture occupying the rooms, but now – empty – it all seemed a very bland, neutral shade.

The first room I came to was the lounge, where the sunlight streamed through the gaps in the blinds to make shadow-stripes on the carpet. They reminded me of a row of coffee Kit-Kats, and this gave me an idea of the cosy conversations I could have here with my new neighbours — sitting next to an oak nest of tables the colour of treacle, wooden coasters, over-sized mugs with steam drifting up lazily.

The dining room, however, was more like milk chocolate than coffee. Maybe that's because it had three small, square windows that made the room slightly brighter, bringing out a paler colour in the carpet than I had found in the lounge. Compared to the dark 85% chocolate cupboards in the kitchen, there was something more-ish about the dining room, like a bar of Cadbury's Dairy Milk that begs to be eaten in one sitting. I could imagine a room as silky-smooth-feeling as this one could be hard to leave, especially if doing so meant a sink full of washing up next door!"

I've taken the task of describing a house, played upon the brown colour in it, and started making comparisons based on various brown foods, all comforting and cosy. Hopefully, the atmosphere of it is that it's going to be a kind of hostess-y, friendly, welcoming place.

You don't necessarily have to use fancy words to make your point. I'm building up an atmosphere by the details I'm choosing to share, and I'm staying focused on this atmosphere. I'm not writing about how one room is yellow and one room is dirty and one room is super huge and glossy, and then going outside in the garden to get distracted by some birds. A description with "cohesiveness" is what I call a snapshot with attitude!

You may find it really difficult to make it all hang together so nicely, but if you simply make a list of important words or related words (say, for a nice house, gleaming, bright, light, shining, yellow, cheerful, solid, fresh), then you can use this list throughout the description to help the whole house have a positive atmosphere. If you want a scary house, you would choose a whole different set of words to put into your details.

DO: Brainstorm a list of 15 words that you would plant in a description of a spooky house.[17]

DO NOT PROCEED
Without doing the task first

Hopefully, you'll see that just a little extra thought about "skin" will be the key skill that separates the mundane from the magnificent!

This technique of making a word cloud that connects is actually a literary device called "lexical field." Basically, lexical field just means word cloud. For example, if I were to list a set of words like this...

- Fire, tripod, sleeping bag, smoke, coals, kindling, air bed, air pump, guy wires, marshmallows, hot dogs, swiss army knife, outside, starry nights

… what is the topic I'm clearly making reference to? Answer at the end of the chapter.

The way I would finish my description of the house is by continuing with the reference to chocolates – something philosophical like:

> "They say that life is like a box of chocolates, but in my case, my house is like a chocolate box! Can't wait to dig in!"

Dr P's View

To me, this should be an easy writing task. It only requires focusing on the topic, using good vocabulary and sentence structures, and controlling your punctuation. So why do students still struggle on this? SILLY MISTAKES, such as:

- Not attending to the topic (memory verse!). If the question is about the city in the early morning, don't write about it throughout the seasons, or walking into the country, or comparing the city in the morning to its night life. Answer the question as it's written!

- The other major problem is over-writing. Students seem to think that piling up adjectives and images is good description, but the meaning of what they write might be total gobbledygook:

"The ratchety branch swayed lovingly in the horrific wind with birds tweeting elegantly like foghorns."

- The biggest mistake by far, however, is telling a story – thinking "video" – instead of describing something like a snapshot. There's nothing wrong with perhaps having a series of three snapshots as you move through the house or walk along the street, but if you start using words like "when" or "then" or "next," "later that day," or even "the next week," then you are probably writing narrative. That is Question 4 or 5; not 2 and 3.

Another issue that "separates the men from the boys" is the mark scheme's expectation of organisation. It calls it "managing beginnings and endings." Students often do fine with their opening, but usually finish their descriptive piece by … well, there's no better word for it … abandoning it. If I'm marking a student's description and start looking for page 2 when there is none, then this piece of work hasn't been successfully brought to a close. Therefore, when planning your description, you must plan your ending. Let's take the example of the house …

how might you bring your description of your new house to a close?

DO: Jot down five ways you can finish a description of a house you go into for the first time.[18]

- *Important Tip: Another challenge with writing a good description is that it's easy to just list things rather than thoughtfully arrange them. You're supposed to be showing off your writing skills, remember? Don't just tell me the stairs go up and the carpet is beige and this room is a bedroom, and this room is a bedroom, and this room is a bedroom (zzzzzz...).*
- *You have to find something to give your description OOMPH! That's why I want you to think in terms of bones, muscles, and skin.*
- *Part of the skill of this question is in choosing the better topic to write about. To me, walking through a house with some kind of atmosphere (other than the obvious s-p-o-o-k-y house) is a rather dull proposition. You have to work quite hard to jazz up your description, instead of listing each room like a kind of inventory. Clearly, the morning in the city is more interesting.*
- *Another observation is that a question will sometimes ask about thoughts and feelings, and students will use this to fall into story-telling techniques. Instead, there are ways to show thoughts and feelings without using a stream of consciousness narrative. For example, if I were to describe a house with gloom and dankness, creaks and groans, and I said I was afraid of every shadow, then I have told you my fears without telling a story.*

- *Most of the marks are impression marking — how well your sentences flow, how interesting your vocabulary is, and how satisfyingly contained your content is. In other words, how much it seems like an organic, thoughtful whole, rather than a mish-mash of random ideas that are being stuffed under a single umbrella.*
- *That said, bad mechanics stick out like sore thumbs. Revise your spelling, punctuation, and grammar as much as you revise past papers. I mean it!*

Finally, a word about variations for Questions 2 and 3. These examples in 0500-31 are very typical; one is about a building, and one is about a place/time.

- Occasionally, you are asked to describe a person. This is a bit more difficult, but it's the same principle: think snapshots with bones, muscle, and skin. Maybe you could write a scene with the person at breakfast, lunch, or dinner. Maybe at home, work, or their hobby. "Spots of time," as the poet Wordsworth would say, rather than a film with a storyline to it.
- Occasionally, you are given bullet points to cover in your question. Remember your GAWPe, and describe according to the bullet point. Maybe you can't really establish an atmosphere in this task, so you can do two things: a) choose the other descriptive question on offer, or b) brainstorm your "lexical field" of words you want to include, and pepper them through your description.

- Just remember: each task is there to give you an opening or a gateway to showing off your writing skills. The exam doesn't really care if you have ever been walking in the early mornings of a city in your own life — it's looking for whether you can describe such a scene in your own words with good mechanics and organisation.

In Lesson Seven, you've learned:

Your 3-step approach to successful description

plan, plan, plan

think, think, think

revise your mechanics

(And add skin to muscles and bone.)

Revision Suggestions from Lesson Seven: Hup-Two-Three

Descriptive Exercises

This exercise can help you add "muscle" and "skin" to the bare bones of a description. I have given you two examples, but you can try your hand at making different atmospheres with the same scene, or find other bland statements from news stories and practise jazzing them up.

Here's a sentence from a news report from a recent newspaper article (remember, news reports are just facts, without "atmosphere"):

"Prince George and Princess Charlotte played in the snow for the first time."

By changing verbs and adding "muscle" detail and "skin" textures, this sentence can indicate different atmospheres of this scene.

1. On holiday in the resort town of Grenoble, Prince George and Princess Charlotte gambolled in the fresh powder like little spring lambs.
2. In the Cairngorms, Prince George and Princess Charlotte prodded the last patch of winter ice with the tips of their fingers, as though it was the peas on their dinner plates that they didn't want to eat.

Hopefully, you sensed in the first one that this was rather a posh place, and the children were having innocent fun in the lovely conditions.

In the second one, the atmosphere was less enchanting. The Cairngorms might be a nice place to ski if you have to, but it's not really a nice-sounding word particularly, and is clearly down-market to somewhere in the Alps. The fact that the children were prodding the ice like yucky peas shows that they're not particularly enamoured.

Final assignment for Lesson Seven

DO: Try writing a bit of Question 2 about the new house. Remember to STOP, LOOK, and LISTEN before you begin writing. Aim for 150 words in the first instance, where you put skin on your bones and muscles. Watch your mechanics! Be careful not to drift into story-telling. It's just a series of snapshots, not a video, so you need to LINGER in each scene instead of darting from room to room. AFTER YOUR 150 WORD OPENING, SKIP A LINE AND THEN WRITE WHAT WILL BE YOUR CLOSING SENTENCE. Ask your parents if the sentence feels like the end or closing of something, rather than just an abandonment.

That list of words in the "lexical field"?

Camping, of course! My friend says, "Cheers!"

Lesson Eight

In this lesson, we're going to turn our attention to Part 2 of 0500-31/32/33, with a particular focus on Narrative Writing usually question numbers 4 and 5. We will be referring to the June 0500-31 paper, so you need to have it in front of you during this lesson.

First, let's review what we did in Lesson Seven.

- We looked at how descriptive writing is a focused/narrow snapshot that tries to create atmosphere through putting muscle and skin onto a skeleton of details.
- We practised important pre-writing steps:

    - STOP-LOOK-LISTEN to really envision and experience the scene.
    - Brainstorm words, phrases, and thoughts

that link to the atmosphere you want to create, such as a "licking doggy" and other kinds of animals who are eating, or a house that's broken, or spooky, or clean, or homely.

- We looked at the question about your new house. You practised stop-look-listen and pictured yourself in a specific place. You thought about how you might choose connected words to give your description atmosphere, and how you would end it without abandoning it.
- I gave an example about a new house that was very brown, but turned it into a comparison of brown colours related to chocolate and such.
- For revision, you were given an exercise about taking bare-bones newspaper articles and adding muscle/skin to turn them into a description with atmosphere.

0500-31/32/33 Part 2, Questions 4 and 5 — Narrative Writing

- Although I love writing narrative stories myself, I have to admit that this task is a lot harder than the descriptive one. That's because there's so much more to think about in a narrative story than in description.
- Descriptive writing wants to establish an atmosphere,

and you do that by putting muscle and skin on your bones.
- Narrative writing needs some description in it, too, but it also adds techniques like characterisation, setting, and plot, including the important skill of creating a climax.
- More about this in a mo ...

There will be two narrative tasks to choose from in the narrative section. One task offers either a set starting point or a set end point (maybe a phrase or an action), and the other is usually more general. What is your GAWPe of this kind of writing?

DO: Jot down in your notebook the GAWPe for narrative writing.[19]

Examiners have shared the following tips for this answer in public Examiners' Reports:

- Remember that stories do not consist of events alone.

- Include realistic details, description, and thoughts and feelings of characters in the narrative.
- Try to write a narrative with a sensible time span that is not too long.
- I would add that most poor answers were episodic rather than well-organised (I did this, then I did that), lacked a good ending, and failed to capture any kind of characterisation.
- Good answers had distinctive and obvious climaxes (even a surprise ending only worked if it were prepared for and not sprung on the reader at the last minute); they were original; and they often included some kind of brief flashback or varieties of time spans. If dialogue was included, it was well-punctuated. Characters seemed realistic, or at least well-drawn.

Question 4 and 5 from 0500-31

Let's turn now to your question paper for narrative writing. Your two choices are to write a story called The Lesson, or a story that ends, "I knew things would be different from now on."

Maybe your brain starts churning up all kinds of cool ideas just by looking at the task, but do take note of this bit of advice from that examiners' reports: the best answers were those which were still rooted in reality, still thought through issues like using the senses, and created characters who were credible. Good answers avoid cliched situations with lots of shooting and violence as though their story were caught up in a written version of a video game, or relationship break-ups that are better suited for anime or soap operas. Those that actually copy the stories of well-known films like The Hunger Games do a huge disservice to themselves — how can anyone cram a 45-minute telly programme or a 220-page novel into 3 pages of a story, and expect it to have any depth, pacing, or beginning/middle/end, except in the most cursory and half-hearted fashion?

There will be some of you will who will nevertheless think this task is a gift – you may be natural story-tellers and in your element when it comes to writing this sort of thing.

Believe me — it is a trickier task than descriptive writing, because not only do you have to be sure to include elements of descriptive writing (creating atmosphere and such), but you have to think through issues like:

- Who is your narrator?
- What's your point of view?
- How do you start in the middle of the action?
- How do you prepare for the end from the beginning (without giving away your punch-line)?
- Who are your characters? (note: you don't want too many)
- What are their motivations? Their obstacles? How will they overcome their problems?

Just like you did for descriptive writing, you need to spend some time pre-writing. You begin both tasks in Part 2 the same way:

- **STOP** panicking and rushing; you need to "breathe in" the scene.
- **LOOK** around your scene.
- **LISTEN** to the surroundings.

Ack! So much to remember!

- *Important Tip: Think before you write; picture your scene; imagine the atmosphere.*
- *Brainstorm! Remember Who, What, When, Where, Why, How to think through some basic ideas.*
- *If an interesting thread begins to appear as you write your story and you want to slot it into the story earlier, use asterisks or arrows to put the idea into it. Not elegant, but acceptable.*

- *Better, however, is to decide these issues in the planning stage! The exam is looking to see if you can organise your writing, so build this skill into your answers from the start.*

I'm going to model the process for Question 4, called The Lesson.

I'm writing this off the top of my head. First, Stop, Look, Listen. (What kind of lesson do I want to learn? Do I want to root it in an episode from my own life, or make something up entirely? It would be more realistic from my own life, so what lesson did I learn? Once I nearly killed my brother by pushing him over as he held an axe, and I thought he'd been killed by it, like a boy in a book I read ... okay ... let's go with that lesson.)

Next, I think through some basic ideas using Who, What, When, Where, Why, How. Okay ... my brother and I were, say, pretending to be the boys in that book. Why? That's what we used to do in the summer, before video games kept kids indoors. The "how" of it – well, we got in an argument about something which I've forgotten, so I'll have to think of a triggering event.

It's a story, so there needs to be a story arc: a beginning, middle, and end. The end is where I push him onto the axe. The beginning is when we go down to the woods with some tools to play backwoodsmen. Middle needs to be the argument we get into.

Perhaps between the push and his turning out to be okay, I need a flashback to the scene in the book I read where that boy is killed by falling on the axe.

I need to establish the game we're playing, the book it's based on, and our ages. Perhaps I could start the story with a reference to the title, so it's clear that I know where I'm going with this episode – it's going to teach me a lesson.

My opening

"I've heard it said in life that truth is stranger than fiction, but there was one time in my childhood days when I wish that truth and fiction had had nothing to do with each other.

The year was 1980. The season was summer — hot, sticky, Texan summer. In those days, my brother and I lived on a farm about ten miles from town, so we spent most of our school holidays on different parts of the ranch, playing make-believe. We used every inch of the fertile black soil, the fishing pond, and the creek bottoms with their crawfish and water snakes.

We headed down that way on one particular morning. We wore jeans we'd specifically cut short to look frayed, old plaid shirts (mostly unbuttoned), and left our shoes at the back door. That day, we were going to be hillbilly boys — like in the book Where the Red Fern Grows — looking for 'coons (there weren't any) and building a bonfire."

As you can see, narrative writing is just as much about establishing atmosphere and using good words and vivid imagery as description is. However, you've got to put in more rising and falling action, you have to have a climax, and you have to consider characterisation and timing.

That's not to say that it's impossible to write a good story; it's just as though there are more balls for the juggler to throw in the air than there are for description. That's why, in my opinion, descriptive writing is easier than narrative — at least in terms of taking this exam.

- *Important Tip: I'm not going to say that you can't do this narrative task, as apparently some schools say to their students. You might get really fired up about the task, and can't wait to tackle it. That's up to you.*
- *What I will say is this: you will need a lot of practice with regard to timing. It's difficult to crank out a story with a beginning, middle, and end, and get all your loose ends tied up in 3 pages. So, if you're going to write the narrative task, you need to practise, practise, practise.*

That's also why, like I did for Paper 22, I suggest starting with the last question and working backwards. Remember our crazy idea from Lesson Four?

I feel as though the writing tasks of Part 2 can offer much more focused, almost formulaic responses, as opposed to Question 1 where the variations are wider (just don't try to shoe-horn an answer from a past paper into a new question; the examiners recognise them and get annoyed). You can allow yourself 35-40 minutes for it, and do a decent job in writing a solid answer (especially a descriptive one which is more focused than narrative to begin with), thus leaving yourself a "whole heap o' time" to tackle that first question, which is no doubt trickier.

Some of you aren't comfortable with this idea, but I just want to throw that out there as an option.

NOTE: If you have liked the idea about starting backwards in your papers – say, with Question 3 in Paper 22, or Question 2 in Paper 31 – then you must practise your mocks and revision backwards as well.

Top Tip:

Here's a good link for IGCSE revision in general, and specifically about narrative writing on p. 14 (don't worry that it talks about coursework and that it's based on the old exam — its explanation about narrative writing is still valid): http://tinyurl.com/lmbmfav

In Lesson Eight, you've learned:

- Narrative writing is like descriptive writing with more balls to juggle.
- The best way to write a successful story is to plan it out carefully before you start to write, so the ending is satisfying.
- The best way to revise for writing a story is to practise a lot of past papers, paying particular attention to your timing. You need to be able to do this within 50 minutes at the most (unless you know you'll receive extra time during the exam).

Revision Suggestions from Lesson Eight: Honing

Revision between now and the exams

- Don't lose sight of your fundamentals:

    - Spend fifteen minutes every day between now and then doing copywork from your chosen book and exposure text.
    - Write down the memory passage four more times before you're done with it.

> - Practise narrating everything you read.
> Write markers in the margins, or as
> notes on a separate sheet of paper.

- Practise makes permanent, so revise practice papers in the same time frame as you'll have in the real exam.
- Stop using the computer and start writing by hand, unless you have permission to use a computer in the exam.
- Start writing with the pen you're planning to use. Black ink is best. I prefer something like a Stabilo fine liner, or a quick-drying gel pen. Both these options make a nice strong line, and the ink flows easily so you don't need to press too hard. Find a brand, size, and style that fits nicely in your hand, rolls smoothly, and doesn't give you cramp. Make sure the ink doesn't bleed through the paper, and that it dries fast so you don't end up with smudges all over your page. You want to give your examiner a nice clean script to read when it's scanned.

Final assignment for Lesson Eight

DO: If you're going to leave the narrative option open for yourself in the exam, you need to get in lots of practice to perfect the timing. Go over past papers and start cranking out stories. Beware of cliches — remember that the examiners like realistic, original work — not derivative or imitative. Try to use episodes from your own life.

Bonus Mini-Lesson

This mini-lesson has only one purpose: to guide you during the 24 hours before you actually sit one of the 0500 papers.

By the time you get to the 24-hour countdown, your revision should be as complete as it can be, especially if you worked your way through this guidebook and took on board the tips, tricks, ideas, suggestions, and advice that have made up the bulk of it.

With just 24 hours to go, your job is two-fold:

- Get plenty of rest, food, and exercise
- Boost your confidence

The first is self-explanatory. The day before the exam, make sure you eat well, go for a long walk, drink plenty of water, and avoid electronics after about 7 pm so your brain can get ready to sleep (screens inhibit the secretion of melatonin, which is your bed-time hormone).

The second can be achieved with a single 30-minute slot of brainstorming. What do you brainstorm? Everything you learned from this guide about the paper you're taking the next day.

For example, when that Paper 0500-21/22/23 gets plopped in front of you the next day, what are you going to find in it? (3 questions; 2 inserts.) Do you have a choice of questions? (No; you answer ALL questions.) What are your strategies for tackling Question 1? (Look back at Lessons 1 and 2, noticing how you should follow the bullet points in your answer; how you need to include 3 layers in the answer as in point, detail, development; and how you read into Passage A to help supply answers for your A3 section.) How many points for reading well, and how many for your writing? What genres might you be asked to write in? Don't forget to pay attention to the italicised description of each piece in the insert.

After you've attended to those two tasks for the day, there's nothing more you can do to improve your chances of a good grade. All the work should have already been done in the weeks and months before.

The best thing you can do now is call your granny (or another dear relative) and tell her you love her. Our loved ones aren't around forever, so it's only natural that we should think of them in our most trying times.

BONUS MINI-LESSON

About the Author

Dr P runs online courses in English for home-educated students who live all over the world. Her 30-week Dreaming Spires Home Learning webinars are structured in a unique tiered format that allows 12-year-olds to get their toes wet with secondary literature, history, foreign language, science, and more, while pushing even the sixth-formers to higher challenges and expectations.

Her Dreaming Spires Revision courses have proved popular since she started them in 2011. While most of her students are UK-based, she now teaches students from over 28 different countries around the world, some of whom have "graduated" from four years of tuition to take up places at Cambridge University and even West Point in the US.

Earlier in her career, Dr P taught in the UK as a secondary school English and Drama teacher, including A-level, and also spent some time teaching university students in the US. More recently, she has been appointed as an examiner in both IGCSE and A-level for the CIE and OCR exam boards.

She has four children, whom she home educates using the Charlotte Mason method. This approach is dedicated to reading lots of good books, analysis, discussion, and contextual exploration, and it underpins the vision for her online courses — which her older children also attend.

In her spare time, she drives her kids to lots of swimming competitions, writes novels, and breeds dogs — her little terriers are native to the UK, a breed known as the English Toy Terrier. They're considered a vulnerable breed because fewer than 100 are registered every year, but being so biddable, loving, robust, and low-maintenance, she finds it surprising that they're not more popular.

Anyway, like this revision guide and the back way she gets to Crufts at the NEC without any traffic, she likes to think of her ETTs as her own little secret.

Appendix A
ABOUT COPYWORK

Have You Ever Considered ...?

Don't you find it interesting that the greatest literary figures in history such as Shakespeare, Tennyson, Dickens, Stevenson, Franklin, Jack London (Oh my, the list is huge...) did not take creative writing or composition courses? Instead, they copied passages from classic literature very carefully, and then tried to write the same passage again from memory without looking at the model. They used their own words when needed, but tried to sound like the original author as much as possible. Eventually, this carried over into their own writing. This is achievable for students today, too. By revising with copywork, their sentence structure will become more sophisticated and their vocabulary will become extensive.

Why Use Copywork?

- Copywork, also called transcription, is a common assignment among Charlotte Mason and classical home-educators.
- During copywork, a student copies a passage word for word, referring back to the original as often as necessary to make sure the reproduction is identical to the original.
- The simplicity of copywork hides the plethora of benefits that this learning method offers.

Copywork is a Language Arts Workout

Copywork has high payoffs, because it deals with almost every aspect of language arts development. It works in a beautifully subtle way. The bottom line is that an understanding of the English language — all parts of it — seeps into the student as they copy the passages.

1. spelling

Careful attention to copying the spellings of words will help develop correct spelling patterns in your student's writing.

2. grammar

A student will likely be copying grammatical structures that they have not yet formally studied. And that's great! Without any formal instruction, the correct grammatical patterns they transcribe will become natural usage for them.

3. punctuation

Who doesn't struggle occasionally with comma or semicolon rules? The beauty of copywork is that the student is repeatedly exposed to excellent punctuation that will slowly become second nature.

4. vocabulary

The rich vocabulary used in the hymns, scripture, poetry, and quotations that you select will be a benefit to your child. Research shows that most students need repeated exposure to a new vocabulary word, used in context, before they can make it their own and use it.

5. composition

The entire writing process benefits from the use of copywork. Besides the elements listed in numbers one through four, the more global elements of composition such as parallelism, style, organization, and literary devices are exemplified in copywork passages. Exposure to great examples gives children models for their own writing.

Some Suggested Books for Copywork

- Pilgrim's Progress, by John Bunyan
- King James' Version of the Bible
- Ivanhoe by Sir Walter Scott
- Watership Down by Richard Adams
- Oliver Twist by Charles Dickens

These are just some options that are viewable/downloadable online. You can use your judgment about other titles if you don't fancy these, but you want the books to be high-quality, literary fiction, and written in prose. These requirements aren't usual for copywork – some people use non-fiction, poetry, drama, etc — but because of the nature of the English exam, you will want to focus on works with long sentences and opportunities for practising how to punctuate dialogue.

Answers and Notes

1. I realise this looks a badly punctuated phrase, but after researching many options for it, I chose this as the clearest, most acceptable option.

2. Remember, mine is only one example of many, so don't feel bad if yours isn't exactly the same. The passage is told from the point of view of Zelda, who is going on a canal boat holiday with her husband, Bob. She clearly isn't impressed by the idea of communing with nature or anything like that, because she keeps trying to get a phone signal instead of listening to instructions for driving the canal boat down the river. She clearly says she would prefer a 5-star holiday and pampering spa-type options, rather than "a tube with windows." Bob, on the other hand, seems ultra-keen.

3. Bob takes Zelda on a canal-boat holiday, but she likes things posh and civilised so she complains all the time.

4. The answer is your own choice, of course, but you could write something along the lines of: "I felt really bad for Zelda. I was listening to the boatman just yak and yak, and didn't even notice that Zelda was so tired. She had been working really hard, so when she wanted to leave suddenly, it just dawned on me how selfish I was."

5. Some of the people I'd have Bob and Zelda meet would be the celebrity couple who have a boat on the canal; or, I'd have them try fishing; or, I'd have them go to the artist's studio and meet the artist; or, I'd have them run into the chap with the dogs again, perhaps with better results this time.

6. The answer is C.

7. "like machine gun fire"

The rain on the canal boat's roof sounded like the rapid, heavy pattering of shots from an automatic gun. The rain is loud and intense; part of a bad storm. By comparing the rain to a machine gun, the author is suggesting that this is an aggressive and violent storm.

8. You might have found the smiling sun, the feathery clouds, the pale blue sky, and the little pearl-like droplets of water. From these clues, you would have deduced a calm, gentle, friendly, peaceful kind of morning.

9. When I did this exercise, I didn't find anything relevant to the question until the third paragraph, and then I found 7 things.

10. The specific parts to circle would be the rain-induced mudslides and the steep angle. If you chose the "unstable

mountain," that's actually a separate point to do with rock issues, more examples of which come later in Passage B.

11:

- A. A letter to a friend = letter, friend, friendly and chatty, inform and share — perhaps persuade.
- B. An interview with your father about his time in the war = interview, father, interested and questioning, explore.
- C. A letter of complaint to your local councillor about broken park equipment = letter, local councillor, probably concerned or aggrieved (but not aggressive), probably persuasive.
- D. A speech to other homeschooled kids about taking up sport = speech, other homeschooled kids, probably like a big brother giving advice, persuasive.
- E. A newspaper article about the closure of a nearby recycling plant = newspaper article, local readership, objective, to inform.
- F. An magazine article about keeping different kinds of pets = magazine article, unspecified but maybe children/young adults/full-time workers, informed/expert, to inform.
- G. A report about the use of swimming pools in your county = a report, perhaps to the council/swim company/parents, informed and factual, to inform.
- H. A journal entry about being grounded = diary, to self, annoyed/perhaps humbled and sorry, to let off steam.

12. The answers are that the insert is an article, probably in a local paper aimed at local people (including teens), an objective viewpoint with the purpose to inform. Your answer is supposed to be a letter of application, written to someone who can hire you for the position. Given this GA, your writerly attitude should be formal but with some humility and tact. The purpose is to be persuasive. Don't forget that it's "e" — an exam!

13. You may have said that you want the job to go on your CV. Or maybe you think it's sad that old people can't shop online, and you want to help them do that. Or maybe you just like being around older people because they have as much to teach you about life skills as you can teach them about computing. Or maybe you would like the extra training that the scheme is offering. Or maybe the article has made you think about what you take for granted and you want to give back to society. Or maybe you even want to show older people that teens aren't all that bad.

14. Answers will vary, but some examples are: a girl in the foreground with light-coloured hair; smiling, looking sideways, holding grass, dark jacket or hoodie; a boy in a shirt with stripes on the sleeves; dog pulling hat; boy trying to get hat; dog is little and black, maybe like a mini Doberman (she's an English Toy Terrier, actually, but you weren't to know that!); the dog wears a light-coloured collar; a younger boy in the background, standing, wearing sunglasses and a hat; the background is hilly with a lake in the distance; ferns nearby; a gate or fence of some kind.

15. Here is one example of how you might have answered this: Bones — a black lamb with a black-and-white-mixed face looked at me; Muscle — a black lamb with a face like an old lady with a bad hair-dye job looked at me; Skin — a black lamb with a face like an old lady with a bad hair-dye job glared longingly through the entrapping fence/seemed to beg me to release him from his pen (or "dared me to take one step closer as though he would bite my legs off.")

16. By the way, I would not be impressed by this description for another reason – how can the viewpoint person know what the laboratory is like inside if the door was obstructing his entrance? THINK!

17. Some ideas: creaky, musty, groaning, howling wind, isolated, dark, dank, cobwebs, a funny chill in my bones, broken things, torn curtains, clanking, banging doors.

18. A few examples of mine: You can leave the house. You can flop down in a room and sigh, being so glad to finally call something your own. You can wonder how you'll ever have enough furniture to fill it. You can make your first cup of tea.

19. Genre is narrative writing; Audience is examiner; Writer will vary, depending on the narrator/persona you choose for the story; Purpose is usually to entertain; finally, "e" reminds us this story is for an exam, so we have to keep within its parameters.

Printed in Great Britain
by Amazon